Gun Violence

Other Books in the Social Issues Firsthand Series:

SOCIAL ISSUES
FIRSTHAND

Gun Violence

Ronnie Lankford, Book Editor

GREENHAVEN PRESS
A part of Gale, Cengage Learning

GALE
CENGAGE Learning·

Detroit • New York • San Francisco • New Haven, Conn • Waterville, Maine • London

363.3
Lankford

Christine Nasso, *Publisher*
Elizabeth Des Chenes, *Managing Editor*

© 2010 Greenhaven Press, a part of Gale, Cengage Learning.

Gale and Greenhaven Press are registered trademarks used herein under license.

For more information, contact:
Greenhaven Press
27500 Drake Rd.
Farmington Hills, MI 48331-3535
Or you can visit our Internet site at gale.cengage.com

For product information and technology assistance, contact us at

Gale Customer Support, 1-800-877-4253
For permission to use material from this text or product, submit all requests online at www.cengage.com/permissions

Further permissions questions can be emailed to permissionrequest@cengage.com

Articles in Greenhaven Press anthologies are often edited for length to meet page requirements. In addition, original titles of these works are changed to clearly present the main thesis and to explicitly indicate the author's opinion. Every effort is made to ensure that Greenhaven Press accurately reflects the original intent of the authors. Every effort has been made to trace the owners of copyrighted material.

Cover photograph © David Sutherland/Terra/Corbis.

LIBRARY OF CONGRESS CATALOGING-IN-PUBLICATION DATA

Gun violence / Ronnie Lankford, book editor.
    p. cm. -- (Social issues firsthand)
    Includes bibliographical references and index.
    ISBN 978-0-7377-4797-3 (hbk.)
    1. Firearms and crime--Juvenile literature. 2. Violence--Juvenile literature. 3. Gun control--Juvenile literature. 4. Firearms ownership--Juvenile literature. I. Lankford, Ronald D., 1962-
    HV7435.G86 2010
    364.15--dc22

                                                      2009038619

Printed in Mexico
2 3 4 5 6 7 13 12 11 10

Contents

Chapter 1: Experiencing Gun Violence

Chapter 2: Speaking Out Against Gun Violence

Chapter 3: Encouraging Gun Ownership

Foreword

Social issues are often viewed in abstract terms. Pressing challenges such as poverty, homelessness, and addiction are viewed as problems to be defined and solved. Politicians, social scientists, and other experts engage in debates about the extent of the problems, their causes, and how best to remedy them. Often overlooked in these discussions is the human dimension of the issue. Behind every policy debate over poverty, homelessness, and substance abuse, for example, are real people struggling to make ends meet, to survive life on the streets, and to overcome addiction to drugs and alcohol. Their stories are ubiquitous and compelling. They are the stories of everyday people—perhaps your own family members or friends—and yet they rarely influence the debates taking place in state capitols, the national Congress, or the courts.

The disparity between the public debate and private experience of social issues is well illustrated by looking at the topic of poverty. Each year the U.S. Census Bureau establishes a poverty threshold. A household with an income below the threshold is defined as poor, while a household with an income above the threshold is considered able to live on a basic subsistence level. For example, in 2003 a family of two was considered poor if its income was less than $12,015; a family of four was defined as poor if its income was less than $18,810. Based on this system, the bureau estimates that 35.9 million Americans (12.5 percent of the population) lived below the poverty line in 2003, including 12.9 million children below the age of eighteen.

Commentators disagree about what these statistics mean. Social activists insist that the huge number of officially poor Americans translates into human suffering. Even many families that have incomes above the threshold, they maintain, are likely to be struggling to get by. Other commentators insist that the statistics exaggerate the problem of poverty in the United States. Compared to people in developing countries, they point out, most so-called poor families have a high quality of life. As stated by journalist Fidelis Iyebote, "Cars are owned by 70 percent of 'poor' households. . . . Color televisions belong to 97 percent of the 'poor' [and] videocassette recorders belong to nearly 75 percent. . . . Sixty-four percent have microwave ovens, half own a stereo system, and over a quarter possess an automatic dishwasher."

However, this debate over the poverty threshold and what it means is likely irrelevant to a person living in poverty. Simply put, poor people do not need the government to tell them whether they are poor. They can see it in the stack of bills they cannot pay. They are aware of it when they are forced to choose between paying rent or buying food for their children. They become painfully conscious of it when they lose their homes and are forced to live in their cars or on the streets. Indeed, the written stories of poor people define the meaning of poverty more vividly than a government bureaucracy could ever hope to. Narratives composed by the poor describe losing jobs due to injury or mental illness, depict horrific tales of childhood abuse and spousal violence, recount the loss of friends and family members. They evoke the slipping away of social supports and government assistance, the descent into substance abuse and addiction, the harsh realities of life on the streets. These are the perspectives on poverty that are too often omitted from discussions over the extent of the problem and how to solve it.

Greenhaven Press's *Social Issues Firsthand* series provides a forum for the often-overlooked human perspectives on society's most divisive topics of debate. Each volume focuses on one social issue and presents a collection of ten to sixteen narratives by those who have had personal involvement with the topic. Extra care has been taken to include a diverse range of perspectives. For example, in the volume on adoption, readers will find the stories of birth parents who have made an adoption plan, adoptive parents, and adoptees themselves. After exposure to these varied points of view, the reader will have a clearer understanding that adoption is an intense, emotional experience full of joyous highs and painful lows for all concerned.

The debate surrounding embryonic stem cell research illustrates the moral and ethical pressure that the public brings to bear on the scientific community. However, while nonexperts often criticize scientists for not considering the potential negative impact of their work, ironically the public's reaction against such discoveries can produce harmful results as well. For example, although the outcry against embryonic stem cell research in the United States has resulted in fewer embryos being destroyed, those with Parkinson's, such as actor Michael J. Fox, have argued that prohibiting the development of new stem cell lines ultimately will prevent a timely cure for the disease that is killing Fox and thousands of others.

Each book in the series contains several features that enhance its usefulness, including an in-depth introduction, an annotated table of contents, bibliographies for further research, a list of organizations to contact, and a thorough index. These elements—combined with the poignant voices of people touched by tragedy and triumph—make the *Social Issues Firsthand* series a valuable resource for research on today's topics of political discussion.

Introduction

Gun violence remains a pervasive problem both in the United States and around the world. Accidents, crime, and war involving guns have a broad social impact that results in the deaths of thousands of men, women, and children each year. Many others are left with serious injuries.

One of the more disturbing trends in gun violence during the past ten years has been the increasing frequency of shootings at private and public schools and colleges. Dr. Robert Needleman wrote, "The last few years have seen a string of unspeakably horrible acts of violence in which children have opened fire on their classmates using high-powered handguns and rifles." Incidences like the April 16, 2007, shooting on the Virginia Tech campus and the Columbine High School shooting on April 20, 1999, have been etched into public memory. While these tragedies occurred in the United States, equally violent school shootings have taken place in other countries. On March 11, 2009, sixteen people were killed in the Winnenden school shooting in Germany.

While school shootings are recognized as a disturbing trend, however, there has been little agreement regarding either the cause or how to address the issue. Ultimately, the issues that have formed around school shootings are the same ones that have formed around gun violence and gun control. On one side, there are those who believe that the easy availability of guns is partly responsible for the problem; on the other side, there are those who argue that people, not guns, should be held responsible for crimes committed. Another issue focuses on the observation that school shootings seem to occur more frequently in the United States than in other countries. There are many theories on why this is true, but as with all issues revolving around gun violence, there is little agreement.

School Shootings and the Law

A number of laws have attempted to address gun violence in schools including the Gun-Free School Zones Act of 1990, which was revised after objections by the Supreme Court in 1995, and zero-tolerance policies. Gun-free school zones made it illegal to knowingly carry a firearm within a thousand feet of public, private, or parochial schools. An individual prosecuted under the act could be fined up to $5,000 and serve up to five years in prison. A zero-tolerance policy states that any student caught carrying a firearm on school property would automatically be expelled. While both policies were broadly agreed upon, many questioned their ultimate effectiveness.

Others have suggested more controversial solutions, including allowing teachers to carry concealed handguns in the classroom. During the 2008 school year, Harold Independent School District in Texas initiated a program that allowed teachers with the proper firearms permit to carry concealed guns. The school district believed that this policy would help prevent school shootings and protect teachers from other violence. As one might imagine, however, placing guns in schools remains controversial. As one parent wrote, "I am all for the right to bear arms, but I am definitely not about to send my children to school where the teachers can shoot!"

School Shootings in the United States and Around the World

Almost any listing of school shootings over the past ten years notes many more incidences in the United States than in any other country. In neighboring Canada, for instance, school shootings are rare. In 2008, there were at least eight school shootings in the United States that resulted in deaths; in Europe, only one resulted in a death; in Canada, there were none in 2008. Many have blamed the prevalence of guns in the United States as part of the problem, but gun ownership is also widespread in Canada. Others have blamed both violent television and violent video games, though both are widely available throughout the world. Finally, some critics blame the United States media for extensive coverage of school shootings. Media coverage raises the possibility that children and teenagers may commit similar or "copycat" crimes.

More recently, school shootings have seemed to increase in Europe. "Europeans might once have viewed massacres at educational institutions as a uniquely American scourge," wrote Bruce Crumley in *Aftermath News*, "but they no longer have that luxury . . ." Over the last three years, incidences in Germany, Finland, and Norway have proven increasingly violent. In November 2007, nine were killed in the Jokela School in Finland; in September 2008, eleven were killed in the Kauhajoki School shooting, also in Finland. As a comparison, in 2008 there were no school shootings in the United States that equaled the number of deaths at the Kauhajoki School. Still, the number of incidences of school shootings in the United States in 2008 was far greater than the number of incidences that have occurred in all of Europe.

School Shootings Today

Ideally, school shootings would be prevented before they occur, perhaps by identifying potential attackers. Many attackers have been victims of bullying, while others have had histories of emotional trauma (e.g., depression, thoughts of suicide). Most are male, and a few have even specifically targeted female victims, as with the shooting and deaths of five Amish girls at a school in Nickel Mines, Pennsylvania, in 2006. Frequently, there are warning signs, often marked by problem behavior. According to a summary of the U.S. Secret Service Safe School Initiative Report, however, "children who attack can be any age and from any ethnic group, race, or family situation. Contrary to assumptions that some of our youth 'just snap'— they don't. They plan." The profile for the would-be attacker, then, is too general to be helpful.

The Secret Service report nonetheless did find one common item that linked two-thirds of attackers in school shootings: they had easy access to guns. Usually, they were able to find guns at home or in the home of a relative. Because of this, many commentators have argued that the root of gun violence in America can be attributed partly to the easy availability of firearms. But Americans remain deeply divided on rights related to the Second Amendment of the U.S. Constitution. Perhaps programs adapted locally, from gun-free school zones to allowing teachers to carry concealed guns, will eventually find broader acceptance. Until then, school shootings will remain a politically charged issue in search of new solutions.

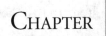

CHAPTER 1

Experiencing Gun Violence

Gangs, Innocent Bystanders, and Gun Violence

Alexandra Shimo

In this article, five people tell the story of how they were affected by gun violence. Mark Farrell was a middleman for drug deals, Brandon Lincoln was a high school student, Giancarlo Tartaruga worked paving parking lots, Gyasi Ferdinand was a crack dealer, and Louise Russo worked as a supervisor for Bell Canada. All testify to one thing: gun violence changed their lives forever. Farrell says that he can never forget what happened because he still suffers from chronic pain related to his injury; Lincoln, shot by an unknown assailant, is afraid that if he leaves his house, he might be shot again; Tartaruga requires both medicine and rehabilitation, but he is afraid that his disability money will not cover his expenses; Ferdinand believes that despite his suffering he is lucky: if his life had continued in the same way, he might be dead now; and Russo feels that her disabilities have distanced her from her family. All of these victims attest to the impact of gun violence on individual lives. Alexandra Shimo, who wrote this article for Toronto Life, *has covered arts and culture for radio and television.*

Mark Farrell, 31

Shot in the back and shoulder on the way to a Black History Month event

When: February 19, 1994

Where: Humber College

Before: Middleman for drug deals and gun sales; sold fake credit card numbers; lived with friends who would put him up for short stints

"It all started when I drove to Ottawa with two people in a stolen car to sell drugs. I went to hang out at the house of one of their mothers while the others went to deal weed. We watched TV together. When they returned to the house, I knew something was wrong. We turned on the news and heard the announcer say Ottawa's first murder of the year had just happened—a robbery gone bad. One of them said, 'Shit, he's really dead.'

"Two weeks later, while I was at an event celebrating Black History Month at Humber College, I was shot suddenly from behind. The bullets hit my shoulder, my back and my spine. I fell into a coma and woke up 10 days later. I wanted revenge, so I asked for my gun and my shoes, but I couldn't move. I didn't realize I was paralyzed. After two months at Toronto Western, I went to rehab for a few months. Then the RCMP [Royal Canadian Mounted Police] arrested me for the Ottawa murder.

"At the trial, the others said I had been with them dealing drugs and had pulled the trigger. Unfortunately, my only witness was my associate's mom, and she couldn't be located to testify. I was found guilty of manslaughter and sentenced to 12 years. In Millhaven prison, I met an ex-Black Panther named Charles Lee Knox. He's a Muslim, and he started giving me religious texts to read. I became more humble. I learned you had to accept the things you couldn't change. Prison taught me how to live and learn. My faith got stronger, and I gained some of my confidence back.

"I appealed my conviction, and my second trial was five years later. The judge stayed the charges against me, and the case was dropped because the judge found the prosecution's key witness completely unreliable. I was finally released from prison on April 10, 2001. I'm now on disability and live in a wheelchair-accessible apartment. Every day, I am reminded of what happened. I am in constant pain—my legs feel like they're being electrocuted. But this doesn't stop me from being grateful for what I have, and trying to better my life."

Brandon Lincoln, 17

Shot in the arm with a shotgun on the way to a party

When: April 17, 2005

Where: Burrows Hall Boulevard and Milner Avenue, Scarborough

Before: Pickering high school student with a passion for football and basketball

"I was at my friend Tony's place in Scarborough. He was playing video games, and I had just dozed off. I woke up after midnight, and we decided to grab some pizza. Tony had heard about a party that was on the way to the pizza place, and he wanted to check it out. Walking there, I was closest to the road. A car drove past, and I saw two flashes. Guns were firing from the front and back seats. Something hit my left arm, and I felt a burning pain. I didn't know why I had been shot, and I was scared it was going to happen again.

"We all ran away from the car, across a football field. We hid in the grass until we were sure the gunmen were nowhere in sight. Then we walked back to Tony's house. We didn't run because we didn't want to make it look like I got shot. If the car came back and saw me, they probably would have shot me again.

"From Tony's house, we called an ambulance, which took me to Centenary Hospital. There, the doctors couldn't take out all the fragments without damaging my nerves. They took out about seven pellets, but there are about 80 still in there. I can move my arm, but if someone bumps into me, it can really hurt.

"I was going to try out for the football team this year, but now I can't. Still, I'm lucky to be alive. If I had been one step back, the bullet would have hit my heart, and that would have been the end of me.

"I don't know who shot me. Sometimes I ask, 'Why me? What did I do? What did I do to deserve this?' I'm still scared whoever it was will come back and shoot me again. So I don't go out as much. I don't tell anyone my address or phone number. I don't hang with the wrong crowd. I keep it safe. It's so easy to get access to guns now. You have to keep watching your back."

Giancarlo Tartaruga, 37

Shot in the spine with a .45-calibre semi-automatic handgun during a robbery

When: January 21, 2002

Where: Escape Cup Cafe, St. Clair Avenue West and Boon Avenue

Before: Paved parking lots and roads during the summer, cleared snow in the winter for the city; main breadwinner for mother (now deceased) and sister

"I was playing poker with some friends. The cafe owner, a friend of mine, had closed so we could gamble in private. It was around midnight. I had just been dealt some cards. Suddenly, three masked men burst through the back door, blinding everyone with pepper spray. The robbers wanted our gambling cash, so one of us dumped it all on the table and said to them, 'Here! Take the money.' One of the masked men was carrying a gun, and he shot at me and my buddy.

"I fell down on the floor, unconscious. An ambulance came, and I was taken to St. Mike's Hospital. At first, the doctors thought I wouldn't survive. I lost a lot of blood, and my liver, pancreas, abdominal aorta, esophagus and spinal cord were damaged. After a seven-hour operation, I was in a coma. For 12 days, my sister stayed by my bedside and prayed. Then I finally came to. I don't remember much, but my sister says I was hallucinating.

"The doctors kept me in rehab for seven months. Now I can't work. My pension and disability payments add up to

$1,013 per month. My sister, Franca, stays home to care for me, and we find it hard to make ends meet. There are medical bills, home adjustments for the wheelchair and the cost of painkillers. It adds up.

"For a while, my legs were getting a lot stronger. I could take a few steps with my leg braces, a walker and the physiotherapist supporting me. But then I started getting pressure sores. I'm prone to them because of my weight. My first was on my behind. We didn't catch it in time—the cavity grew to four centimetres wide and eight centimetres deep, and it became infected. For three months, I had to lie on a special bed in the hospital recovering. Since I returned home, I have had two more pressure sores where I sit. The problem is, I can't begin exercising again or do any physiotherapy until I am sore free. I just have to lie at home and wait."

Gyasi Ferdinand, 31

Shot in the stomach and elbow with a 9 mm handgun

When: May 9, 2000

Where: In a car parked at River Street and Gerrard Street East

Before: Crack dealer; lived with his girlfriend at Black Creek Drive and Jane Street

"My friends and I used to sell drugs from Church to River Street and Carlton to Queen. I was known as J9, because my gun was a 9 mm. If we caught anyone dealing who wasn't authorized by our gang, we would rob him. Sometime in 1994, I found an outsider selling crack on our turf, so I took his drugs and cash. Six years later, I found myself standing next to the same guy in the washroom of a Queen Street club. I said, 'Remember what happened between you and me? Let's just let bygones be bygones.' He pulled out a gun and pointed it at my head. Then he asked me, 'Why did you remind me of that?' and pulled the trigger.

"I don't know what happened—maybe it was the grace of God—but the gun jammed. I grabbed it, and we wrestled on the floor. When the club's bouncers burst into the room, the man ran off. Knowing my reputation, he probably figured he had to kill me, and I knew I had to kill him. A week later, I was hanging out with a friend . . . smoking pot and drinking. I heard a rap on the window and looked up and saw the man with a 9 mm. One bullet struck my right elbow, one caught my left index finger, and two hit my stomach. I didn't feel much at first, then I started coughing up blood and I thought I was going to die. My lung had collapsed, my liver was damaged, my intestines were punctured, and a kidney had to be removed. I lost so much blood that my tendons didn't get enough oxygen and shortened. I was in a coma for six days. When I woke up, I couldn't open my hands.

"While I was in hospital, a friend of my mom's came to my bedside with a pastor from the Church of Jesus Christ the Apostles Foundation and a few other church members. I had a vision that I was being embraced by a figure in white. It felt great, and I started crying. At that moment, I decided to give my life to God. Since then, I have learned the Scriptures, and I became a minister. Now I preach at their church at Vaughan and St. Clair West. I go to schools and teach children about my life and how I've changed. I still have difficulty moving my fingers and need another operation to fix my hands and one to fix the wall of my stomach. But all in all, it's a good thing that I was shot. Otherwise, I might be on the streets, or in jail, or dead."

Louise Russo, 47

Shot in the chest and spine with an AR-15 rifle

When: April 21, 2004

Where: California Sandwiches, Chesswood Drive and Sheppard Avenue West

Before: Worked for Bell Canada, supervising orders; wife and mother of three (Steven, 21, Krista, 16, and Jenna, 18, who has congenital myasthenia gravis and global delay; she cannot talk, walk by herself or feed herself)

"Krista and I stopped off at California Sandwiches on the way home from Air Cadets at Downsview Park. Krista stayed in the car while I went in. It wasn't very busy, and I remember saying to the young lady at the counter, 'This will be quick. I'll just be in and out.' Then I heard a strange sound. It was like a vooom. I thought someone had rammed into my car, and my first concern was for Krista. Then I heard pew, pew, pew, and I remember my hair moving. My first instinct was to get down. But they were firing an assault rifle, and I didn't make it. The bullets are called mushroom bullets, and they break and ricochet. It was horrible. My right hand felt sticky—it was my own blood. I couldn't open my eyes, and I couldn't hear anything. Then I realized I was dying. The first thing I said to myself was, I can't die. I can't, I can't. Who's going to take care of Jenna?

"When I came out of a state of shock, I felt the coldness of the floor and wanted to check on Krista, but I couldn't move. My body was shaking, and I was in intense pain. One bullet had ricocheted inside of me, breaking two ribs, collapsing my left lung and shattering my spine. Another bullet had grazed my skull, slicing off a clump of flesh, and my head was burning. I was frantic and terrified, so I started crying out, 'Krista! Krista!' over and over again. When Krista finally came in and saw me on the floor covered in blood, she screamed, 'Mommy!'

"I was in hospital and rehabilitation for eight months, but I didn't regain any feeling in my legs, and I'll be in a wheelchair for the rest of my life. I'm on a lot of medication for the pain. I have a burning feeling across my chest where the paralysis starts, and then I feel nothing. My circulation has gotten much worse, so I get chronic infections. My disability affects my marriage. It's traumatized my husband, Sam. Also, my daughter Krista has become more timid—she panics now when her dad leaves her in the car to run an errand. I'm unable to take care of my children. I can't even dress Jenna or feed her. It's been an incredible loss. But we take it day by day and do what we can. My family and friends, and the community's support, have helped pull me through."

Accidentally Shooting My Best Friend

Kemp Powers

In the following excerpt, journalist Kemp Powers recounts how when he was fourteen years old, he accidentally shot and killed his best friend. Powers lived with his mother in a small Brooklyn apartment. When he was twelve, she took him to the firing range so he could learn how to shoot the weapons she kept at home. When his mother was at work, Powers often brought his friends home, and sometimes they would play with the guns. One day when playing with his mother's .38, Powers, believing the handgun was unloaded, pointed the gun at his best friend and pulled the trigger. For a moment after the flash and explosion of the gun, the world seemed to move in slow motion. Only slowly would Powers realize what had happened.

When I was fourteen, I shot my best friend in the face and watched him die. I'm not trying to sound cold when I say it like that. I'm not a criminal, at least not to the people who matter. Not to my family. Not to his family. Not to my friends. Not even to the state of New York. Still, just typing these words shocks me; I see them taking shape across the screen, and I can't believe the actions I'm describing are my own. In the fifteen years since it happened, I haven't discussed the incident in detail with a single person.

Henry was one of seven homicides that day in New York City. At fourteen, he wasn't even the youngest—a twelve-year-old from Queens held that distinction. But his was the death I saw with my own eyes, the one I caused with my own hand, the one I will carry for the rest of my life.

Kemp Powers, *The Shooting: A Memoir.* Cambridge, MA: Thunder's Mouth Press, 2004. Copyright © 2004 by Kemp Powers. Reprinted by permission of Thunder's Mouth Press, a member of Perseus Books, L.L.C.

Henry and I met through a mutual friend in seventh grade, and we got along from the start. We both stood out from the crowd. He was unusually broad and muscular for a twelve-year-old, and I was so tall and skinny that every school gym session brought on a round of jeering comparisons to Manute Bol, that seven-foot, seven-inch twig of a basketball player from the Sudan. Henry and I were as physically different as two teenagers could be.

Within just a few months of that first junior high school year we were close friends. We walked together to the subway station every day after school, we read comic books and we shared a hatred for the bullies from nearby John Jay High School, who'd tease us and show up on Halloween to rain rotten eggs, batteries, and water balloons on us. We talked about things in a way our other friends couldn't understand. We were best friends.

Home was a tidy two-bedroom co-op on the second floor of a small brick building in the Kensington section of Brooklyn, a typical border neighborhood populated by Hasidim, Eastern Europeans, blacks, and Puerto Ricans. Our small apartment was a source of pride for my mother, who'd raised my three older sisters and me single-handedly since splitting with my father when I was four. I occasionally saw and heard from Dad, but he was mostly a stranger in my life.

Mom worked full-time as a nurse at an old-folks home fifteen blocks from our apartment and was also a captain in the Army Reserve. She kept four guns in the apartment. Her military background, combined with an interest in firearms, had turned her into something of a collector. One of her guns was an antique flintlock pistol. I called it the cowboy gun because it reminded me of the huge, heavy revolvers Clint Eastwood wielded with such cool authority in those old spaghetti westerns. The cowboy gun was strictly a collector's item. She also kept a .22 caliber semiautomatic rifle (with a scope), a .25 caliber semiautomatic pistol, and a .38 caliber snub-nosed revolver.

When I turned twelve, Mom took me on my first trip to the range, where I had a chance to try out all the guns. The .22 rifle, with its glossy wood stock and endless barrel, had always struck me as being pretty. At the range, I found that it was easy to use and very accurate, thanks to the scope. But the low caliber made me feel like I was firing a BB gun.

The .25 pistol was my favorite. I loved that it was small and silver and looked almost like a toy, with a loop of dingy white masking tape wrapped around the handle. I loved the tiny five-shot clip. I also loved that it had less kick than the .38, which made it a good range gun, easy to fire with accuracy.

The .38 was the intimidator. The fact that it was a revolver played right into all my fantasies. Anyone who'd seen *Taxi Driver* knew what a snub-nosed .38 looked like and what its reputation was. "The .38, that's a fine gun," the dealer told Robert De Niro as De Niro aimed and pointed it out the window. "You could hammer nails with that gun all day, come back, and it would still cut dead center on target every time." The one in the movie was silver with a pearl grip. Mom's was service-style, black metal with a brown wooden grip. It felt much heavier in my hand than the .25—which I took as a sign of its power. It felt dense. It kicked hard when I fired it. Mom kept it just inside her armoire near a box filled with bullets. It was the gun she kept handy for personal protection.

When Mom wasn't around, I taught myself to spin the .38 on the tip of my index finger like an Old West quick-draw artist. I showed off all three guns to my friends and even let them handle them. They'd come by after school, in the hours before Mom got home from work, and we'd play with the guns. By freshman year in high school, Henry was a regular visitor. We'd started going to different schools, but he'd hop the F train right after classes let out, and he'd be waiting for me in front of my building by the time I got off the bus.

On the afternoon of April 14, 1988, Mom called from the nursing home where she worked to say I wasn't allowed to have any friends over that day. "I just want to come home and get some rest," she said, explaining she was exhausted from all the work she'd been doing lately. "Okay," I said, and hung up the phone, failing to mention that Henry and another friend, Chris, were already on their way over. Not to worry, though: Mom wouldn't get home until 5:30 or so, which would give us plenty of time to hang out. They'd be gone before she even set foot in the apartment.

When Henry and Chris arrived, we went straight to my bedroom. Henry dropped his backpack and coat onto the floor and plopped down on my bed. Our apartment was a one-bedroom unit when Mom bought it, but in an effort to give me some privacy (my three older sisters having moved out), she had erected a wall with a door in the living room to create a second bedroom for me. To compensate for the wall's blocking out sunlight to the now smaller living room, my bedroom walls weren't built all the way up to the ceiling, instead yielding about twelve inches of space, enough to let a sliver of light through. I loved that room. I kept the walls white, free of posters—I'd moved around enough to know that removing a favorite poster from a wall would only result in its destruction. I used a couple of large pillows to dress my bed up like a sofa so friends would have a place to sit and hang out. It made my room feel like my own little apartment.

I can't recall how the .38 came out. I was probably just showing off Mom's gun again. By this time, I'd been to the range several times and had mastered my index-finger spin, so I fancied myself somewhat of an expert. I'd even devised a game where I would insert a bullet into one of the chambers, spin the cylinder and then lock it into place for a game of Russian roulette. In reality, I'd either palm the bullet and discreetly drop it onto the floor, or place it a few notches away from the chamber so there was no bullet in the barrel when the trigger was pulled. I can't even count how many times I pointed it at my head, at walls, at friends, and pulled the trigger to their shock and subsequent amusement. It was something I thought I was good at. It made me feel tough.

Anyway, with Henry and Chris sitting on my bed, I started my routine. First I demonstrated the index finger spin. Then I pretended to insert a bullet randomly, spun the cylinder, and pointed the gun at Henry. I smiled and pulled the trigger, ready to shout "Gotcha!" after making him flinch. Only instead of the dull click of the hammer followed by laughter, there was a deafening explosion and a flash of light. The smell of gunpowder filled my room. Chris and Henry turned away, their backs to me, and my initial thought was that I must have just fired into the wall. The silence was complete. In the endless second after the gun went off, it was as though everything was moving in slow motion.

The Day I Was Shot

Frank Gardner

In this essay Frank Gardner explains that when he was assigned to cover a story in Saudi Arabia, he believed that there was little danger of being assaulted by terrorists. The country, however, had changed drastically since his last visit; now, the relative openness of the Saudi landscape had been replaced by a number of protective measures. Still, Gardner believed he would be safe, and proceeded to travel to Al-Suwaidi to learn more about the growth of terrorism in Saudi Arabia. In Al-Suwaidi, he was approached by a man who at first appeared friendly and then pulled out a gun. Gardner ran, but was shot twice; a second group of terrorists shot him a number of times as he lay on the ground. He remained still, playing dead until his attackers left. Gardner recalls his feelings of isolation as his calls for help went unanswered for a half hour, when the police finally arrived. Gardner is a journalist and the author of Blood and Sand: Love, Death and Survival in an Age of Global Terror, *from which this excerpt is taken.*

"Do you have time for some supper?" called Amanda from the kitchen. I looked at my watch. It was Tuesday June 1 2004 and the car taking me to Heathrow airport would be here in 20 minutes, but I was packed and ready to go.

"I'll be right down," I replied, and walked out of our top-floor bedroom, unaware that that was the last time I would ever see it.

Three days earlier there had been a bloodthirsty raid by Al-Qaeda fanatics in the eastern Saudi town of Al-Khobar. The terrorists had found a prominent British expatriate,

Michael Hamilton, shot him dead, tied his body to their car bumper and dragged it around town in some kind of grisly parade of their power.

Then, masquerading as government security forces, they had marched into a residential complex housing many westerners, Indians and Filipinos who worked in the vast oil industry. Rounding up all those they suspected of being non-Muslims, according to the testimony of survivors, the militants coolly slit the throats of the "non-believers". By the time order was restored, 22 people had been killed.

A New Assignment

Saudi Arabia's charismatic ambassador to London at the time, Prince Turki al-Faisal, had wasted no time in touring British television news studios to defend his government's record in tackling terrorism. A former Saudi spymaster, Prince Turki was unusually open and frank. He encouraged British journalists to visit, helping with visa requests. I was to go there for BBC [British Broadcasting Corporation] News with Simon Cumbers, a freelance Irish cameraman and trusted veteran of countless assignments.

Amanda and I sat up talking late that night. My wife was understandably anxious; clearly there were people on the loose in Saudi Arabia who hated westerners with a passion.

"Do you have to go to Saudi?" she asked. I did not. Unlike some other networks, the BBC is quite reasonable about asking people to go to difficult places and I have never been told the equivalent of "Go to Baghdad or pick up your P45" [British term referring to termination of employment]. But Saudi Arabia was not considered a high-risk country like Iraq or Afghanistan; I knew of no visiting journalists who had ever been threatened there.

"Then are you taking a flak jacket?" asked Amanda. This was a touchy subject between us: she has always maintained I had agreed at our wedding never to be a flak-jacket journalist, a pledge I have no recollection of making.

Leaving Home

In truth I have never seen myself as a "war correspondent", believing that no story is worth getting shot for, although there are occasions when it is wise to wear a flak jacket as a precaution. But I did not feel this was one of them: no civilians wore flak jackets in Saudi Arabia and if anything it would only attract unwelcome attention.

Amanda's concerns troubled me, however, not just because I did not want her to worry while I was away but because she has an uncanny knack of being right about places she has never even been to.

"So what are you going to say when terrorists have got a gun to your head?" she asked me.

I tried to reassure her—and myself—that we were going to tread extremely carefully. We would put ourselves entirely in the care of our Saudi minders, and knowing how over-cautious they tend to be our only problem should be not getting enough access to interesting subjects.

One of the last things I packed was a miniature copy of the Koran, one of several I keep to give as presents to hospitable Muslim hosts, a gesture that always brings great appreciation.

I kissed my wife and children goodbye and watched them recede through the car's back window on that warm summer night. I tried to dismiss the feeling of unease, reminding myself that I had been to Saudi Arabia countless times and that I'd always felt safe there.

Soon I was at Terminal 3 with Simon. He and his wife Louise had their own freelance production company, and Simon had recently felt bad about asking one of his cameramen to go to Baghdad. He had resolved that he would take the next filming trip to the Middle East.

A New, Dangerous Saudi Arabia

I remembered Al-Khobar as a quiet, dull place. There was no entertainment and little for expatriate westerners to do other than drive across the nearby causeway to freewheeling Bahrain.

When we reached the Al-Khobar Meridien, I could hardly believe it: there was a sandbag gun emplacement outside, backed by an armoured car. I had often stayed here in my former incarnation as a Gulf banker, but even during the dark days of the Gulf war in 1991 there had never been anything like this atmosphere of brooding tension. I had only been away 11 months and already this was not the Saudi Arabia I knew.

The next few days passed in a whirlwind of filming, driving and frantic editing in our hotel room, followed by a dash up the motorway to the nearest satellite uplink station in time to make the one, six or 10 o'clock TV news in Britain; in other words, pretty much typical of a foreign news-gathering trip following a big event.

In the middle of this schedule I was invited to attend the memorial service for Michael Hamilton. I sat at the back, as discreetly as I could, taking notes for the report I needed to file for the Radio 4 six o'clock news. I had never known Hamilton, but I was overwhelmed by the sadness and futility of his death. One had only to look round the room at his mourners to judge his popularity: Saudis, Britons, Bahrainis and Indians had all come to pay their respects.

The British ambassador, Sherard Cowper-Coles, read a tribute and that night we interviewed him in his hotel room, sharing my packet of Walkers shortbread fingers. He had a refreshing tendency to tell it how it is.

"Saudi Arabia does have a serious problem with terrorism," he said, "and I predict there will be more attacks on westerners." Prescient as he was, he could not have foreseen that Simon and I were to be Al-Qaeda's next victims.

Government Red Tape

On the Friday, the day off in Saudi, we took the short flight to Riyadh and spent the afternoon at a barbecue with British expatriates in their walled compound. Life here had recently taken a turn for the worse, they said.

They had accepted for some time the risk of being caught up in a suicide bombing but now there was a new horror: being executed in cold blood on the basis of one's religion or the colour of one's skin. The expats had heard reports of Al-Qaeda scouts marking westerners' numberplates with chalk as potential targets.

There was a chicane of concrete roadblocks outside our Riyadh hotel, but there was no visible armed guard on duty and this worried me. If Al-Qaeda decided to enter, I did not believe there would be much to stop them.

In my room I went over to the window and decided that if there was an armed raid I could probably jump down on to the tree below, which would break my fall. I felt that a raid was unlikely, though; the summer heat meant there were so few western guests in the hotel it would hardly have been worth Al-Qaeda's time.

Simon and I wanted to report how the Saudi authorities were combating the country's Al-Qaeda-inspired terror cells. We spent a morning traipsing round the ministry of information, applying for permission to film. Saudi Arabia does not allow unescorted film crews, partly for their own safety. Many Saudis are deeply suspicious of foreigners with cameras, convinced they are trying to film their women or pass the footage to some western government.

We asked to film three things: checkpoints and other physical security measures; an interview with a senior counter-terrorist official; and a general view towards Al-Suwaidi, a restive area of south Riyadh where there had been a shoot-out six months earlier between police and an Islamist cell leader, Ibrahim al-Rayyes, who had been killed.

The ministry of information was not encouraging about our requests and—as Arab government ministries close at 2pm—we went back to our hotel for lunch and a swim, planning to fly home the next day. I took a call from BBC2's Newsnight, asking me if we could stay on, but I said we were reluctant to hang around in this tense atmosphere when we had nothing firmed up to film.

Traveling to the Interior

So it was somewhat to our surprise that permission came through in mid-afternoon to film around Riyadh, including the district of Al-Suwaidi. Reluctantly—because we had mentally finished our trip—we roused ourselves from the pool and went up to our rooms to change.

I watched a few minutes of the D-Day 60th anniversary celebrations on television, admiring the veterans in their berets and medals and pleased that my father had made the trip back there with my mother.

We piled our camera gear into a government minivan. Mubarak, a black Saudi, one of thousands of Arabs with African ancestry, was at the wheel. Beside him was Yahya, our assigned "minder" from the ministry. I had never worked with him before but he assured me immediately that he was an old hand at chaperoning foreign film crews.

Yahya seemed very easy-going and far more eager to help than most of the government minders I have encountered in the Arab world. We were free to go wherever we chose in Riyadh, he said, but we could not film checkpoints.

We asked to go straight to the edge of Al-Suwaidi and drove south through the suburbs of Riyadh. They were unremarkable to look at: low, whitewashed, flat-roofed buildings, usually above a row of shops selling cold drinks, fabric and spare car parts.

People were just starting to emerge on to the streets after the mid-afternoon siesta; a few of the men, I noticed, wore the short robes and long beards of devout fundamentalists. Here and there was a neon-lit fast-food joint, a sandy backstreet, an overflowing litter bin. One could sense this was a poorer part of town, but the poverty was not extreme.

When we drew up on the edge of Al-Suwaidi it looked exactly like every other residential housing area I have known in the Gulf states: villas surrounded by high walls topped by purple bougainvillea. Patches of flat stony wasteground separated the buildings, and while there was some graffiti on the walls there were also several expensive four-wheel-drive cars parked in the shade.

The Appearance of Safety

The area was now calm, we had been assured, but still we had no wish to go into it, only to film from a distance to give the viewer an impression of what the place looked like.

There was not a soul around, although after a while some laughing children appeared and wanted us to film them. Simon got me to do what is known as a "walking piece to camera", one of those earnest, strolling soliloquies from the reporter that is supposed to set the scene in context, or at least prove to the viewer that the reporter has been there.

Simon and I had agreed in advance that we would spend no more than 10 minutes here, but Yahya was very relaxed and certainly there was nothing to suggest any kind of threat—no furtive figures darting into doorways, no twitching curtains—so we did several takes from different angles to get the filming just right.

Again and again I strolled across the wasteground towards the camera, pausing to deliver my words and point out the villas in the background where police had traded fire with militants six months earlier.

After about half an hour we were on the verge of packing up when a car pulled up close to our minivan. I was vaguely aware of some people in the distance, but when a young Saudi got out of the car there was nothing suspicious about him at first.

Like every adult male Saudi, he wore the traditional white thaub, essentially a smart shirt that extends all the way down to the ankles. He looked very young, perhaps still in his teens, and had a kindly face with a hint of a smile, almost as if he knew us or our two Saudi escorts. Was he coming to ask directions? Perhaps he knew the driver and had come to chat.

Looking straight at me, he called out, "Assalaamu aleikum" ("Peace be upon you"). All over the Arab and Islamic world this is the traditional Muslim greeting, a reassurance to a stranger that you wish him no harm.

I replied with the standard response: "Wa aleikum assalaam wa rahmatullah wa barakaatuh" ("And upon you the peace and the mercy of God and His blessings").

A Surprise Terrorist Attack

The man paused, a curious look on his face, then with no sign of haste he reached his right hand into what must have been a specially extended pocket sewn into the breast of his thaub. I did not need to see the weapon to know what was coming next. It was like a film with a predictable ending.

"No! Don't do this!" I shouted instinctively in Arabic.

He pulled out a long-barrelled pistol. Oh my God, I thought, this cannot be happening.

I ran for my life, sprinting away from our van and into the deeply conservative quarter of Al-Suwaidi. There was a loud crack behind me and I felt something sting my shoulder. I didn't know it then but the bullet passed clean through, hitting the shoulder bone on the way.

My adrenaline must have been pumping because I remember it being no more painful than a bee sting, and I ran on, trying to put as much distance as possible between me and the gunman. For a few brief, happy seconds I thought I was actually going to make it, trusting in the power of my legs to outrun my attackers.

I felt almost euphoric at the prospect of escaping them, and I began to look ahead for cover. There was not much. Everywhere I looked there were high, windowless walls, locked doors and wide open spaces. But it was academic; I never made it that far.

There was another loud bang and the next thing I knew I was down on my front on the tarmac, felled by a bullet in the leg. I had run slap into the terrorists' second team; they had overtaken me in a minivan to cut off my escape. Now they were crowded inside the open sliding door of their van while I lay prone and helpless on the ground, looking up in horror at this group of Islamist gunmen.

They appeared very different from my first attacker; they had made no attempt to disguise their jihadi appearance. Their thin, pale faces were framed by wispy, unkempt beards in the style of most extremists and they had the look of people who spent all their time indoors.

Instead of the neatly arranged headdresses with a sharp crease in the middle worn by ordinary urban Saudis, these men wore theirs wound tightly round their foreheads like a bandage. It was the isaaba, the dress worn by jihadi fighters who consider they are about to go into battle, the same style worn by the 9/11 suicidal hijackers in their video testimonies and by Mohammed Siddique Khan, the leader of the July 7 London bombers, in his posthumously released video warning to the West.

I realised then that I was doomed. These men were no casual, have-a-go amateurs; they were the real thing, a hardcore Al-Qaeda terror cell bent on attacking their government, killing westerners and "cleansing the Arabian peninsula of infidels".

In that instant I glimpsed faces driven by pure hatred and fanaticism. I pleaded with them in Arabic, as so many hostages have done in Iraq, while they held a brief discussion as to what to do with me. It did not take long. They responded to my pleas by opening fire once more.

Life-Threatening Injuries

Even then it crossed my mind how unfair this was. I had spent four years studying Islam for my degree, learning Arabic, reading and translating the Koran and other Islamic texts. I had lived happily among Arab families, fasted with Bedu tribespeople in Jordan, taught English to the impoverished family of an Egyptian taxi driver in a verminous Cairo slum.

For the past few years I had tried hard to explain the complexities of the Middle East and the thinking behind the Al-Qaeda phenomenon to western and international audiences. And this was my reward? A bunch of bullets in the guts from men who had convinced themselves they were killing in the cause of Islam. It just did not seem right.

From somewhere close behind me a gunman stood over me and pumped bullets into the small of my back, hitting my pelvis and sacral bones and causing immeasurable damage to my internal organs. I don't remember it hurting at the point of impact, just a deafening noise each time he squeezed the trigger and a sickening jolt as the bullets thudded into my guts. Each time he fired it was as if a giant hand had picked me up and slammed me down on the tarmac. It rocked my whole inner body frame, like the chassis of a car in a head-on collision.

Bloody hell, I thought, I'm really being shot. I'm taking a lot of rounds here. So is this where I float gracefully up into the sky and look down at my body sprawled out below? What an idiot you are. You're supposed to report on Al-Qaeda, not get so close to them you end up getting killed!

There was one thought in my head that overrode all the others. I have to survive this, I told myself, for the sake of Amanda and my girls. I cannot leave them on this earth without a husband and a father.

Playing Dead

I closed my eyes and kept as still as I could, face-down on my front. The shooting had stopped and there was a discussion going on in Arabic. One of the terrorists was getting out of the van and walking towards me.

I held my breath, playing dead while I listened to his footsteps drawing closer. I felt a hand reach into the back pocket of my trousers and remove Simon's radio microphone (which they left at the scene). Then he fished into the other back pocket and took out that miniature copy of the Koran that I had remembered to pack in London.

There followed a terrifying few seconds when any number of horrors could have been inflicted on me. In the previous week this same cell had dragged Michael Hamilton's lifeless body from the back of their vehicle. Would they now be tempted to do the same to me?

The week after the attack on us an American helicopter technician, Paul Johnson, would be kidnapped in Riyadh and beheaded, his captors filming his execution then keeping his severed head in the family freezer for days until it was discovered in a police raid. I have no idea if the Koran in my pocket saved my life or if the terrorists were by now convinced they had finished me off.

For me, lying punctured and bleeding on the ground, there suddenly came the sweetest sound in the world: the noise of my attackers revving up their engine and driving off. They were leaving me for dead. There followed total silence. No wail of sirens, no crying of children, no clatter of approaching feet.

Waiting for Help

Ominously, there was no sign of Simon, the minder or the driver either. It seemed I was completely alone. Why wasn't anybody coming to my rescue?

I felt many things at once: I was relieved and amazed to be still alive, I was furious at the injustice of this attack, yet I was surprisingly calm. I waited until I thought the coast was clear then I flipped over on to my back, supporting myself half upright with extended arms so I could call out more effectively for help.

As I turned I felt my legs roll over like two dead logs, my feet flopping flat and lifeless against the ground. My right leg was bent in and out at crazy angles and I could feel nothing below the waist.

"Damn," I remember thinking, "that's not good. If I survive this I'm going to need some serious physiotherapy." Unseen by me, someone was discreetly photographing me with a mobile phone and this was the grainy image that appeared in newspapers and on TV within hours.

By now the adrenaline had worn off and I was in the most excruciating, indescribable pain. The clean white shirt I had pulled on an hour ago for the piece to camera was saturated in blood. I had lost count of the number of times I had been shot.

In a cracked and desperate voice I cried out in Arabic for help. My cries were of base, animal pain. I was emitting sounds I did not even recognise.

At first no one came; the place was deserted. Then a handful of local Saudi men drifted on to the scene and my heart leapt. With their straggly beards and loosely wrapped headdresses they looked disturbingly like the people who had just shot me. Had they come to finish me off?

Before I had time to think about it they were joined by a dozen more locals. Despite the pain, I felt reassured by the crowd, which was now getting sufficiently large that if anyone was carrying a concealed weapon he was unlikely to pull it out in front of so many witnesses.

"Nobody Came to Help"

And then the strangest thing happened. Nobody helped me. In Muslim society, charity and hospitality are legendary. I have known Egyptians cross four lanes of rush-hour traffic to help with a flat tyre; an Omani minister once gave me his prized walking cane inscribed with his title in silver; Indonesians have slaughtered their sole goat to share with me. And yet here I was, lying in the road, obviously very badly injured, and yet nobody came to help.

That is one of the things I remember most: the terrible feeling of loneliness, the sense that I was completely on my own, that I could not rely on anyone to help me. I was obviously an object of interest: there was plenty of discussion and pointing at the empty cartridge cases that lay all around me. But something to staunch the blood? A pillow? A glass of water? Even a few words of comfort? Forget it.

The only charitable explanation I can think of is that perhaps nobody dared come near me lest they get dragged off to the police station as a witness.

Staying alive became an endurance test. I feared that if I blacked out and lost consciousness I would be dead by the time I reached hospital, so I willed myself to stay alert.

I had never considered myself to be particularly tough (I have always been a complete wuss about cold showers), but I had had some experience of endurance challenges, having run two marathons at university and completed Hong Kong's 100km MacLehose Trail in under 24 hours. But this was different, it was like nothing I had ever known in my life. Bizarrely, I remember thinking, "Ah, but Frank, you have never given birth and that must be quite an ordeal."

Help Arrives

When the police finally showed up after about half an hour, alerted by somebody in the neighbourhood, they joined a growing throng of people all gawking at me from a distance. It was strange that in years of broadcasting I had never felt self-conscious, despite knowing that millions of people were watching. Yet here I was, being closely observed by 30 or so people, and it did not feel good.

By now I had lost a lot of blood. I was still conscious, but there was no sign of an ambulance or any medics; the policemen seemed unsure of what to do with me.

Somebody asked me if I had noted down the numberplate of the attackers' van. I think I replied that I had been too busy getting shot to notice, but I did tell them I was British. I knew that Britain was almost as unpopular as America in some quarters here, because of the Iraq invasion, but I hoped that someone would get word to the British embassy.

Several khaki-clothed policemen manhandled me into the back of their patrol car. Aware that I was a bloody mess of broken bones and gunshot wounds, they laid me lengthways on some kind of plank contraption. They did the best they could, but the length of my body was greater than the width of their car. And so I remember my head and shoulders protruded ludicrously from one of the back windows.

The police car drove off at speed, sirens blaring, lurching initially over rough bumpy wasteland. I had no idea where they were taking me, but I was in too much pain to care. On top of the agony the bullet wounds were causing me, I now had to grip on to the roof of the car to stop my head getting knocked about.

We pulled up at last at the Al-Iman hospital—not, I learnt later, one of Riyadh's finest. There was a huge commotion at the doorway as everyone argued how best to extract me from my rear compartment and on to a hospital trolley, while I lay groaning and writhing but still conscious. At one stage I was being pulled in opposite directions.

I was rushed through the hospital doors and into the operating theatre. My last memory was of looking up at the faces of the surgeons. They wore an expression close to panic. Then my pleas for painkillers were answered. A needle slid into my arm and I sank at last into oblivion.

Surviving a
Near-Fatal Gunshot

David and His Mother, Louise

In 1996 David's brother accidentally shot him when the two brothers were playing with their father's gun. The following selection presents perspectives from that day by David and his mother, Louise. At the time, David was seven years old, and following the gun blast, he remembers lying on the floor, thinking how he needed to go to school. His injuries, however, were serious, and he would not remember the first six surgeries he underwent to repair his body. David's mother hurried home from work after learning of the accident, and encouraged him to fight for his life while he was in the hospital. The doctor in attendance noted that the shotgun slug injured David's kidney, colon, small intestines, and pelvic bone. It would take David seven years and eighteen surgeries to return to a resemblance of normal life.

*T*he end of the gun hit our couch and the gun went off

David: "We were in the house waiting for the school bus to come. Me and my brother got one of my dad's guns out. He had gone hunting that previous night and he did not unload the guns or put the safeties on, he put it in the gun cabinet and he didn't lock it. He left early that morning. Me and my brother got the gun out; I was looking at it. My back was toward my brother, he took the gun away, and when he did he lost his balance and fell. The end of the gun hit our couch and it went off, it went through the glass in the gun cabinet and then it hit me, in the back, on my left side. I knew I'd been shot, I just didn't think it was that bad. I just laid on the floor while my brother went to get help. I thought he went to

Stephanie Arena, "David," *WoundedinAmerica.org*, March 3, 2009. Wounded in America is the sole copyrighted material of writer Stephanie Arena. Reproduced by permission.

school until he walked back in. I was thinking, my mom's going to kill me if I don't get on the school bus. I remember them coming in with the stretcher. I remember waking up in the hospital. I don't remember the first six surgeries, but I remember the rest. I try not to think about it. Things aren't too bad. I don't exactly have a normal life; I really don't know how it changed my life."

All I saw was the gun cabinet door open, broke

Louise (David's Mother): "The boys were alone. I went to work at 4:30 that morning. Ryan called me at work and said, 'David's hurt and it's bad.' When I got home I didn't know what happened. I just went to the kitchen; if I'd gone all the way around I would have seen all the blood on the floor. All I saw was the gun cabinet door open, broke. I thought, he got cut by the gun cabinet. I never dreamed he was shot. They did the first surgery, then they med-flighted David to Columbus [Ohio]. He was still bleeding inside. When he got to Columbus they had to do another surgery, because his artery was still open. He was in ICU [intensive care unit] for four days and then they put him in a regular room and he couldn't walk or eat. One day he was waiting for an MRI [magnetic resonance imaging], I was standing there holding his hand, and he said, 'Mom, I'm just going to give up, I'm too tired to fight anymore.' I said, 'You're not giving up. I come in here with you and we're going to walk out together. You're going to get well.' It took us seven years, but he's well."

It opened him from his belly button back to his spine

"The bullet was a twelve gauge deer slug. If you can look at a seven-year-old, about sixty-five pounds, it opened him from his belly button back to his spine. It took out his kidney, half his colon, twenty percent of his large and small intestines, his pelvic bone was broke and his hip bone. It damaged the abdominal wall. He can't hold his arm up over his head because they had to cut out muscle under his arm and attach it to his hip to protect the intestine. It took two years for everything to grow back. He has a very thin line of skin over his abdomen from his belly button to the middle of his back. When good skin did grow back, having no muscle there, when he would walk, that intestine was just rubbing against his thin skin. He can take gym only if he has a turtle shell around him, if he gets hit the wrong way he could die. His colon hasn't healed since the accident. So far he's had eighteen surgeries and another one's scheduled."

CHAPTER 2

Speaking Out Against Gun Violence

Remembering My Son and Working to Prevent Future Tragedies

Michael Steber's Father

Like many active fourteen-year-olds, Michael Steber enjoyed the outdoors and sports. He was also well liked and had a number of friends. One October day during a storm, Steber went to a friend's house for shelter with a number of others. His friend took out one of his father's guns, shot the gun from the back deck of the house, and, believing the gun chamber was empty, fired another round into the house. The bullet hit Steber and killed him instantly. His parents tried to understand the tragedy, and in trying to do so, found themselves involved in the Peace Action Council and other firearms organizations. Through these organizations, they worked for legislation on both the state and national levels in hopes of preventing future tragedies.

Michael was a typical, energetic, healthy, active 14-year-old who loved the outdoors, building forts in the woods, building castles on beaches. . . . He loved nature, wild animals and once even kept a pet rabbit hidden from us in his bedroom. He loved the environment, hiking in the woods, swimming in the ocean or climbing to tops of mountains. We did a lot of family camping, starting out in tents, then graduating to a pop-up camper that we took to various state and national parks. Mikey had an easy ability to make new friends and to be a friend to both man and animal.

The phones were always ringing and the front door slamming with new friends bounding in and out. He was constantly expanding his horizons, he'd go to dances to meet new

"Gun Victims Memorial: Michael Steber," *Brady Center*, March 3, 2009. All information © 2009 Brady Campaign to Prevent Gun Violence. Reproduced by permission.

friends. He even was asked to a "Ball" by an older girl—we had to get him a new shirt and sport coat. He wasn't even out of eighth grade!

He loved to try any new sport, but he especially liked wrestling and lacrosse (his favorite). He was an altar boy and Boy Scout, had run for class president. Mikey wanted to play a role in making our world a better place to live.

One day, the same outdoors that Mikey so loved forced himself and three friends inside because of a hard rain. The boys had been playing football and decided to move indoors to be safe from lightning. Ironically, the house they ran to for safety was a house with six loaded, unlocked guns. That day I made a big batch of chicken wings and told them to come on over to watch Syracuse play Penn State as soon as the rain stopped. That day when Mikey left our house in his Syracuse Lacrosse sweatshirt to play football would also be the last day we saw him alive. October 14, 1989.

A Deadly Accident

Simple safety measures and trigger locks would have saved Mikey's life that day. The house Mikey and his friends ran to for shelter was owned by a man who did not practice safe gun ownership, did not store his guns properly and set a bad example for his son by being careless and reckless with firearms. His son, taking cues from his father, was equally careless. Finding one of his father's guns, he and another boy went out on the back deck and fired a round into the river that flowed behind the house. Coming back inside, he pulled the clip out, and, wrongly thinking the gun unloaded, pulled the trigger. The gun fired. A bullet had still been in the chamber. It struck Mikey as he watched TV in the living room. He died instantly.

The power had been off at our house, and we were sitting in a living room lit by candles. We wondered where Mikey was, when the power suddenly came back on. Almost simultaneously, there was a knock on the door. It had been a weird day to begin with, starting sunny but ending in the black darkness of a rare October thunderstorm. When we answered the door, what had been an eerie day became one of sheer horror and sadness.

A chaplain escorted by two police officers quietly informed us that Mikey was dead. The news left me numb. I could not believe what I was hearing. We went to the morgue, hoping that perhaps the police had the wrong description. Looking through the glass at the morgue, my mind drifted back to when he was a newborn, lying in the hospital bassinet, sleeping peacefully. Disbelief and reality clashed as the mind struggled with the heart.

Seeking Answers

Questions clouded my mind. How could this have happened to him? To us? How could I survive the battlefields of Vietnam, only to see my son die of a bullet? Why wasn't it prevented? Was a law broken? What laws are there to prevent this from happening to someone else? I started asking all these questions to our local newspaper editor. He gave me all the information he had on the groups directly involved with tragedies like ours. That's how I was introduced to HCI [Handgun Control, Inc.], the Center to Prevent Handgun Violence and the Educational Fund to End Handgun Violence.

We started out by writing editorials to our newspaper; we got all kinds of phone calls in response—both supportive and nasty. As our resolve grew, we wrote even more letters, held community meetings in school auditoriums, churches, anywhere, to anyone who would listen. We got involved with more grassroots organizations such as MOMS (Mothers of Murdered Sons), New Yorkers Against Gun Violence and others. We went to the state capitol in Albany to rally for stronger child-access prevention laws. We wrote and phoned our elected leaders constantly.

These tireless efforts, along with the efforts of Congress-
man (now Senator) Charles Schumer and Representative Caro-
lyn McCarthy (a firearms violence survivor herself) produced
the Children's Gun Violence Prevention Act of 1998. Thanks
to their efforts and that of Senator [Pat] Moynihan and President [Bill] Clinton, the climate is right for pushing for tougher
laws to prevent the kind of tragedy that took Mikey from us.

The Personal As Political

A lot of hard work by people becoming more vocal in their
local communities is helping change attitudes and mindsets
across the country. We've received strong support from HCI
and the Center to Prevent Handgun Violence. Together, we've
been able to promote gun safety at both a local and national
level. Locally, we continue to speak out and we work closely
with groups that share our goal of protecting our children
from senseless gun violence. These include pediatricians, emergency room nurses, DAs, police departments, and scores of
others.

Together with the local Peace Action Council, we produced a video entitled "Echo of a Gunshot." Our story was
featured in HBO's "5 American Handguns, 5 American Families." We also have created a Citizens Task Force for Gun Safety.
The task force's mission is to promote gun safety awareness
among parents, teens and youth. With the staff at the State
University Hospital of New York, we produced posters with
the theme "Guns, Lock 'em for Life." We distributed these at a
legislative rally in Albany.

In the short run, we'd like to see a CAP [child-access pre-
vention] law passed in New York. In a broader sense, we'd like
to have the Children's Gun Violence Prevention Act passed in
Congress to prevent tragedies like the one that took our son's
life. We also want gun manufacturers to change their attitudes
about gun design. We want guns sold with the owner's safety

in mind. A trigger lock or a chamber load indicator could have saved our son's life. A simple redesign or trigger lock is a small investment in safety.

A $7 trigger lock is nothing compared to the cost of choosing a coffin and tombstone for your child. Parents should be carving out their child's future—not carving their child's name in granite.

Perhaps we could establish a monument, a memorial in Washington, D.C., dedicated to all the children who have died of gunfire. A national day of mourning could be set aside for these children. Perhaps we could make it May 30. As a nation, our focus during Memorial Day is less and less on the veterans. Perhaps we could bring a new meaning to Memorial Day by remembering the children who have died of gunfire.

Testimony of a Virginia Tech Parent

Andrew Goddard

On April 16, 2007, Andrew Goddard's son Colin was shot four times at Norris Hall at Virginia Tech. In the following testimony to a panel at George Mason University, Goddard describes sitting in the hospital beside his son, who was hooked up to multiple machines and tubes. He relates that although it is impossible to understand the events of April 16, he did know for sure that the young man who had injured his son had done so with an easily obtainable firearm. Indeed, he points out, even when one looks at events like the tragedy of 9/11, many more people are killed by firearms over time. Unlike 9/11, though, no one declares a national emergency or declares code red for firearm violence. Goddard concludes by urging the panel investigating the shootings at Virginia Tech to take whatever measures are necessary to ensure that what happened on April 16, 2007, never happens again. Goddard is the president of the Richmond Million Mom March.

My name is Andrew Goddard and my son Colin was shot four times in room 211 of Norris Hall at Virginia Tech. I stand before you today ready to take you to a place that no one else may choose, or be at liberty, to take you. I want you to sit beside me in the hospital room on that Monday night with my son.

I want you to look at him lying there with all the pipes, tubes and wires of modern medicine connected all over his body. I want you to listen to the beeps and whirs of the machines that are working to help his body overcome the multiple shots. I want you to look at his face and see perhaps

Andrew Goddard, "Testimony of a Virginia Tech Parent," *Freedom States Alliance*, March 3, 2009. Reproduced by permission.

your own child or a loved one and feel with me the helplessness of being a parent that can do nothing for their child at that moment. You will learn, as I did, that bullet wounds are not sewn shut, due to risk of infection, but left to bleed. I want you to watch, as I did, as blood oozes from the five holes in his body, soaking the dressings, his pillow and his bed sheets. You will learn, as I did, that bullet fragments lodged in his body are not routinely removed and that they will stay with him for life, as will the huge titanium rod driven down the full length of his femur to stabilize the fracture. I wanted to take you to that bedside to remind you of the suffering of the survivors, I will leave it to others more qualified than I to take you to the place from which the majority of the other victims will never return.

Starting that night, and for almost every day since, I have conducted my own internal investigation into the event, as any parent would do. I asked myself a million times, how did this happen to my son and why? I still have no concrete answers other than that this awful tragedy was the direct result of the interaction between a deranged individual and two simple, efficient and readily available killing machines.

Guns Equal Violence

As to the motive for the actions of the killer, I have no idea, but the method that he used to carry out this heinous act is much easier to understand. Despite what others have said, my son and the other victims were not in the wrong place at the wrong time. My son was in the right place, a classroom of a well-respected university at 9:00 am in the morning. What place could have been righter? Despite what others may tell you, the fact that Cho was able to purchase his weapons so easily is a serious indication of the problems that exist with gun control in our country and especially here in Virginia.

On September 11, 2001, Al Qaeda terrorists carried out the most horrifying attack on U.S. soil ever, killing more than

3,000 people in several locations. The government sprung into action and we as a nation were warned about the imminent threat to our lives posed by Al Qaeda. Many new laws and various pieces of legislation were enacted to keep us safe from this hideous threat. The government even installed a color-coded alert system to keep us informed about the level of threat that these terrorists pose. I believe it is currently yellow.

Since that same day in 2001 at least 60,000 of our fellow citizens have been killed in gun violence, which represents a rate of killing of more than 20 times than that inflicted by Al Qaeda. A rate of killing that they could only dream about, yet we are still unable or unwilling to review our legislation on gun control.

Members of the panel, if such a thing existed, then today the National Security Threat Level for gun violence would be at level RED which would represent the highest level, or in other words "absolute certainty of attack." At least the same number of our fellow citizens will die from gunfire today as died at VT [Virginia Tech] on April 16. Indeed the number may be considerably higher. Sadly the level was also RED the day before the VT attack, the day of that attack, the day after the attack and every single day since. It is red today, it will be red tomorrow and will remain that way until we come to our senses and take some concrete action to protect ourselves from this needless slaughter.

Security on College Campuses

Yesterday I visited VT and was given a tour of Norris Hall by one of the police officers that investigated the incident. I was very impressed by his knowledge and the professional way that he dealt with my questions. I also saw the first signs of changes that the university is making in light of the knowledge learned from the attack. One specific example was the replacement of the original bump bar door locks with new flush-mounted locks that cannot readily be chained together to corral victims into a killing zone.

Why do I ask you to consider the fine details? It became clear to me yesterday that the difference between me sitting here with my son and me sitting with the other parents of the deceased victims can be measured not in yards or feet, but in fractions of an inch. The difference in response time that meant the difference between life or death can be measured not in hours or minutes, but in mere seconds!

You as a panel need to examine all the aspects of this tragedy, as the eyes of the world are on you. When you finally make your report, you will have the ears of the world too. Please examine the minutia of this event, but don't be afraid to look at the big picture items also. The future security of American campuses and other locations is in your hands.

Confronting the Gun Industry

Bill J.

In 1997 a sixteen-year-old boy named William was held at gun-point during a robbery of a fast-food restaurant where he worked. Even though William followed the gunman's instructions, he was shot and killed. Following his son's death, William's father became interested in the gun industry and how it had changed since his own childhood. He notes that whereas gun dealers and manufacturers had once shared a vision of social responsibility, they now seemed happy to sell firearms to anyone. As he met with other people who had also suffered a loss, he gradually realized that gun manufacturers are uninterested in the well-being of the people who buy guns. He concluded that the gun industry was only interested in making money.

My sixteen-year-old son William was shot and killed in 1997 at a fast-food restaurant where he was working. He was on his second day at work, and he was where he was supposed to be. He had this brand-new job, and he was very excited about it. A man caught William as he was coming out the back door, and grabbed him from behind and put a semi-automatic handgun up to William's neck, and he told William to open the door.

William turned around and knocked on the door, the manager was still inside. She looked through the peephole and saw William standing there with somebody behind him with a gun up to his neck, and she realized that this was really a very dangerous situation, and so she opened the door, did exactly everything we tell people to do when they have this kind of confrontation. And as soon as the door was unlocked and opened, for whatever reason, the man shot William through the neck and killed him.

Bill J., "My Son William," *GunStories.org*, March 1, 2008. Reproduced by permission.

The guy was caught five minutes later by the police and he's now serving a life sentence without parole in Virginia for the murder.

The New Gun Industry

I grew up around rifles and shotguns—my dad hunted with his brothers. My uncles and my cousins went out hunting, I didn't particularly want to learn how to shoot animals, but I clinked cans with a .22 and BB guns and learned how to shoot in Boy Scouts—a pretty normal boyhood life out in the country. And one of the things that I started to realize as I was looking into the gun industry after my son was killed, was that this wasn't my father and grandfather's gun industry anymore. It had changed.

I had always sort of implicitly trusted firearms and the people that sold them, and then I began to realize that with this whole new subculture of violence that's been propagated throughout our culture and our society, that gun dealers don't care. They just don't care. The manufacturers don't care, the people that sell them don't care, and if I were to write a letter to the people that made the gun that killed my son, I'd get a letter back saying, "Well we're really sorry about what happened, but it's legal for us to make these guns, it's legal for us to sell these guns, we're going to continue to do so, so leave us alone." That's their attitude.

I became very disillusioned and I realized that there are a lot of questions that I did not know existed about the gun industry. And as I got connected with other gun violence survivors, these questions start to arise, and you start finding out things. And so, our response to that is, "Oh my gosh, that's nuts," and we get involved with other victims, we get involved with victims' organizations.

Changing the Gun Industry

And I'll guarantee you one thing, we do not go to the NRA [National Rifle Association] for solace. We do not go to the gun manufacturers with our grief. We go to people who understand and to people who can help us move forward. And typically that takes a form of activism, where we begin writing letters to our legislators, we begin working on legislation, we begin testifying for good gun laws, we begin getting involved in organizations and donating to organizations like the Brady campaign.

But even then we are in a very difficult position because the gun industry is a multi-billion dollar industry. And that's just buying and selling new guns, that doesn't include the camouflage clothing, the accessories, the holsters, the hunting clothing and all of the magazines that are out there everyday spreading their propaganda about how wonderful it is to own a gun and how every man, woman, and child should have the right to do so. I used to read *Field and Stream* when I went to my grandfather's house and I sat there and read all the articles, you know it wasn't any of this propaganda garbage that you're seeing today.

One of the things that we are deeply distressed by now that my wife and I have become far more involved and more informed about the gun industry is that the gun industry really doesn't care about the people that buy their firearms. They don't care about the blood that's spilled; they don't care about what's going to happen to that firearm after it's purchased. They are in the business to make money.

SOCIAL ISSUES
FIRSTHAND

CHAPTER 3

Encouraging
Gun Ownership

Carrying a Concealed Handgun

Bob Owens

Bob Owens started with a simple idea: what would it be like to carry a concealed handgun for six months? In this selection, he describes the process of applying for a concealed handgun license and then contacting several companies for the equipment he would need for his test: guns, ammunition, and holsters. In the beginning, Owens found carrying a gun somewhat awkward, and there were a number of places—such as his daughter's elementary school—where he simply could not carry a gun. He also practiced using his guns at the shooting range to make sure that he knew how to use them properly. While there were a number of adjustments to make, in the end, Owens found that carrying a concealed gun every day was no different than carrying his wallet. Carrying a gun, he believed, was finally like wearing a seatbelt: while one never planned to get in an accident, it was good to be prepared. With a concealed weapon, Owens believed that he would be able to protect himself if he was ever in danger. Owens is a contributor to Pajamas Media.

I spent Super Bowl Sunday this year learning that I should always be nice and polite and have a plan to kill everyone I see [in a North Carolina classroom, where I took a concealed-carry class].

On May 13, I was awarded my concealed carry permit and decided to carry a handgun as often as I was legally allowed, where I was legally allowed, for as long as I felt like doing it. I was interested in finding out what it felt like to carry a gun, what was the best way to carry, and if the various legal hurdles would make it so impractical that I'd simply give up.

I was also curious about how carrying a gun might change the way I looked at the world. Did the mere act of carrying a gun mean I was paranoid? Would carrying a gun *make* me paranoid?

I was about to find out the answers to all these questions, but first I needed equipment in the form of guns, holsters, and ammunition. I contacted Smith & Wesson and told them of my plans, and they generously arranged to ship me a pair of handguns for a lengthy testing and evaluation period.

Guns and Ammo

One was a M&P9C, a compact 13-round (12 in the magazine, one round in the chamber) 9mm semi-automatic pistol designed to be a backup weapon for police officers, or a primary weapon for concealed carry. Compact, black, and all business, it certainly looked capable of playing the role I intended for it.

The other handgun they sent was a new twist on an old classic. For years in television and in the movies, police detectives always carried snub-nosed .38 revolvers. The five-shot, aluminum-framed 637 revolver they sent me came with the bonus of a Crimson Trace (CT) laser mounted in the gun's grip. When you grabbed the revolver with a firm grip, the laser projected a menacing red dot where the bullet would impact, in both daylight and the pitch black of a moonless night. The 637 included a keyed internal lock on the left side of the frame that blocked the cylinder from opening and the hammer from being cocked.

DeSantis stepped up and provided me with three different kinds of holsters to use. The neoprene Nemesis pocket holster was designed to work for those who carry in coat or deep pants pockets. The Cozy Partner is a classic, well-finished, inside-the-waistband holster that provides an excellent compromise between accessibility, security, and concealability. Both of these holsters were made for the 637CT revolver. For the M&P9C semi-auto, I went with a high-tech holster made of Kydex, the DS Paddle, and a single magazine pouch made of the same material for the spare 12-round magazine.

As for cartridges for these guns, ATK and Winchester took extremely good care of me, providing hundreds of rounds of CCI Blazer and American Eagle practice ammunition to test these guns, and their high-end Federal Premium Hydra-Shok, Supreme SXT, and Silvertip premium defensive ammunition.

Several days later I got the call from my gun shop that my handguns had arrived. I went to pick up the M&P and the 637CT, and things got tough. I learned the first day that deciding to carry is the easy thing; finding where you can *legally* carry is the hard part.

A Typical Day

My typical day started by taking my older daughter to her elementary school, dropping my infant daughter off at her daycare, and then driving to work on a corporate campus in Research Triangle Park. In none of these locations is concealed carry permitted; if I'd been armed, I would have managed a trifecta of felonies before my first cup of coffee. The 637CT, which I'd planned to carry in the pocket holster with the intimidating Winchester Supreme SXT hollowpoints, stayed at home. Some experiment this was turning out to be!

It was a couple of days later that I finally had a chance to legally carry, when my wife dispatched me to the local pet store chain to pick up various kinds of critter food for the Owens family menagerie. As it turns out, a J-frame revolver with a full grip like that of the 637CT doesn't fit real well in anything but the large side pockets of the cargo-style shorts I was wearing, so with every step, the 637CT slapped against my thigh. It was annoying, to put it mildly. Minimal clothing was required to deal with the heat with any degree of comfort, so the pocket holster, paired with a revolver with a full-size grip, was off the carry list until it was cool enough outside for a jacket.

Likewise, I quickly found that the DS Paddle holster that carried the M&P was impractical for me based upon what I wore in the summer. While the Kydex holster was very fast on the draw and very comfortable to wear, my normal summer attire of shorts and short-sleeved shirts simply couldn't cover the gun from view. I was learning through trial and error that the style of holster that works for you will largely be decided by how you dress. It was becoming painfully obvious to me that to carry the handguns I had with my summertime wardrobe, only an inside-the-waistband (IWB) holster would keep the business end of the gun hidden, with the butt of the gun held up tight against my side for concealment under an untucked shirt.

Luckily, DeSantis had already shipped me a very good holster for the revolver in the Cozy Partner. It was well-made, comfortable, and held the gun securely even when I bent over to pick something up. Unfortunately, I didn't have an IWB for the M&P, so I made it a point to do what so many folks do, and went to try to find something relatively inexpensive to do the job.

The holster I chose from the Holster Store was their Pro Carry Deep Comfort, which was almost half the retail price of the comparable DeSantis holster. While the fit was fine and the stitching was strong, the Pro Carry was not finished as well on the inside as was the Cozy Partner, which had an interior that seems to have been sanded almost completely smooth. Until it was broken in, the Pro Carry's rough suede interior finish shed fibers of leather (and leather dust) nearly every time it was drawn. Several times early on, the M&P wouldn't release cleanly with the front sight snagging. After some time passed and the excess material worked its way out or was worn down, the holster became serviceable and I still use it today. That said, I wish I had put the money upfront for a better-finished holster the first time around, which would have saved myself both time and uncertainty.

A Trip to the Shooting Range

I learned all of this in just the first few days of carry. All the while I was self-conscious and occasionally uncomfortable; the weight of the 637CT riding behind my right hip felt odd, and I imagined the bulge it created was huge. During this time I was constantly reaching back to make sure that my shirt wasn't pulling up and leaving the butt of the gun exposed. As I learned that my shirt wasn't riding up and got used to the idea of carrying, the self-consciousness started to fade away . . . a little.

It wasn't until day nine that I was actually able to find the time to take both guns to the range for a solid workout. Yes, we all know that every gun expert on the planet will tell you to shoot your firearm at the range and get used to it before carrying, but let's be honest: people don't always do as they should. I had some previous experience with five-shot snubbies and carried the 637CT for the first eight days because I thought following the first rule of a gun fight was more important than not having a gun at all.

At the range, I learned several things about the 637CT very quickly. First, the factory did a good job calibrating the Crimson Trace laser in an almost perfectly parallel plane to the barrel, and the gun was very accurate. My first three shots fired single-action (hammer manually cocked first) at a human silhouette clustered in one ragged hole just an inch up and inch to the left from the glowing red dot projected onto the target at a distance of 10 yards. Confident in the accuracy of the laser I turned it off to focus on working with the fixed sights, firing 2–3 rounds of 158-grain American Eagle lead round-nosed bullets at a time.

While the 637CT is a joy to carry because of its lightweight aluminum frame, the weight reduction and carry comfort come at the price of stinging recoil, even with the full-sized rubber grips that came on the gun. After 50 rounds, my hands were stinging. It was not a pleasant experience, but then these guns aren't designed to be given heavy workouts. By their nature, snub-nosed revolvers are to be "carried a lot and shot a little." I loaded the Winchester SXT +P hollow-points, figuring the hot 130-grain bullets would exit with more flash and recoil than the 158-grain practice loads, but was pleasantly surprised. The difference in recoil was negligible, and the flash, if anything, was reduced. A box of SXTs went quickly and accurately through the target five yards away, and I was ready to put the 637CT away and try its semi-automatic cousin.

After shooting the lightweight revolver, the polymer and blackened stainless steel M&P snapped out 9mm bullets with recoil that seemed like that of a .22. I fired multiple strings at three, five, and seven yards, going through 150 rounds of aluminum-cased Blazer 9mm in no time at all. I then loaded and fired 20 rounds of Federal Premium Hydra-Shok personal defense ammunition—once again noticing the high-end ammo seems to produce less flash—and called it a day. The 240 rounds of centerfire ammunition were as much as I could handle in one session.

Summertime Peace of Mind

Throughout the heat of the Carolina June I found myself gravitating towards the M&P for carry in most situations where I was allowed to carry, though late-night runs to the store found me reaching for the 637CT because of the laser. Carrying a weapon was far from routine at this point, but I was far less self-conscious about carrying. It was also during this time that my carry class instructor's "have a plan" speech began to make sense. Before I began carrying, I would be thinking about one issue or another as I carried out errands for my wife and kids, and couldn't have told you much about what was going on around me. Because I was armed I felt a greater responsibility to be aware of my surroundings, noting where I was and who was around me. I wasn't planning to kill anyone, but I was making sure that I minimized risk by being aware of what was going on.

By July, I was carrying the M&P almost exclusively. I'm more familiar with semi-autos and tend to shoot them better as a function of having more experience with that kind of firearm. It also wasn't prohibitively heavier than the 637CT, held more than twice the ammunition, and could be reloaded far more quickly. Granted, the ammunition capacity issue isn't a factor in most real-world shooting situations—criminals aren't special forces soldiers and tend to break off their attacks at the first sign of lethal force—but knowing you have additional ammunition on hand if needed is comforting.

In August, however, one feature of the 637CT really stood out.

While on a family vacation in South Carolina (North Carolina has reciprocal licensing with many other states), I carried the 637CT because gun safes did not exist in the beachfront condominium we rented, and I wanted to make sure that there was zero chance that the gun could be reloaded or accessed by any of the children or unqualified adults present. Smith & Wesson builds a version of many of their handguns with a keyed internal lock, and the 637CT was equipped with this option. After I arrived and unloaded the SXT hollow-points, I put the ammunition in my luggage and the 637CT in the carrying case it came with, with the keyed action locked, and placed it upon a high shelf in the bedroom closet. I didn't have to worry about any potential accidents and the peace of mind was reassuring.

Concluding the Test

My testing and evaluation period was coming to an end, and I'd either need to return the handguns to Smith & Wesson or buy them. Somehow, my wife just couldn't understand why I *needed* more than one handgun at a time—much in the same way she couldn't understand why I needed more fishing rods or why the spouse of a golfer can't understand why their fanatic needs yet another wedge—and so I had to make a decision. I would have done well with either, of course, but I went with the M&P because of my familiarity and confidence with that kind of gun and the relatively inexpensive cost of 9mm ammunition when compared to other centerfire rounds. If I had grown up shooting revolvers, I have little doubt that I would have chosen the 637CT.

As the weather began to cool in September and October I was able to start wearing heavier clothing and the Kydex DS Paddle came out more. Unlike the IWB holsters that I wore tucked inside the waistband of my pants behind the hip, the DS Paddle is worn outside the pants and it hid well under a sweatshirt or light jacket. The heavier clothing also made it easier to carry the spare magazine in the Kydex single magazine carrier on the belt, where it would be easier to access should I ever need it. Also in late September I completed my web contracting gig at the corporate site that forbids handguns, so I was free to carry almost every time I went out.

By mid-October, after almost six months of carry, putting on my holster seemed as natural an act as picking up my keys and wallet before leaving the house. The weight on my right hip was hardly noticeable, the slight pressure vaguely comforting. I was no longer self-conscious and am far more aware of what is going on around me. That awareness, in and of itself, makes me far less likely to walk into a questionable situation where problems may arise.

Carrying a concealed weapon hasn't become a chore or an obsession. It is simply something I do now, like putting on my seat belt when I get in a car. I never plan on getting into a wreck, but the seat belt is always there to protect me. The M&P compact plays a similar role. Although I hope I never have to use it, I can be confident that it is there to protect me if I ever need it.

Unlearning Gun Prejudice

Tricia Shore

Although Tricia Shore had grown up around guns, she believed that guns were for hunting, not for protection against the government. She explains in this selection how while attending college, she discovered that it wasn't considered politically correct to like guns. She also, however, met her husband in college, a Libertarian and a proponent that guns were an important protection against governmental power. While Shore thought little about these issues at first, she began to see that the government regularly interferes—often illegally—in people's lives. She now feels the Second Amendment espouses rights that are as important as any other rights granted in the Constitution, and unless citizens arm themselves, there is nothing that can stop the government's growth of power. Shore lives in Los Angeles where she homeschools her three children.

The well-educated, homeschooling, breastfeeding mom at one of the Southern California homeschool park days that we attend, has summed me up as a libertarian. I use the small "l" variety only because I've yet to register as an actual Libertarian: "I like what I've read about Libertarians," she told me, "but I have a problem with the gun thing."

Uh-oh.

"The gun thing" is something that I thought I understood until I met my capital "l" Libertarian husband over ten years ago. "Guns protect us from the government," he told me, which I thought at the time was a statement made only by anti-government freakish types. I now respect such supposed freakish types much more than I used to. In any case, I thought he was really nice and that he'd make a great father.

Three children later, I still think he makes a great dad and I'm even more fond of him these days, but my ideas on the gun thing have changed.

Growing Up with Guns

I grew up in rural North Carolina, close to the mountains, where almost everybody hunts. Indeed, everybody has a gun. When supposed gun safety advocates tell us that our guns should be behind twelve or fourteen locks and placed in a high corner that is only accessible by ladder, I smile. Gun safety at the house I grew up in consisted of saying, "That gun can kill you; don't touch it." Those eight words were all I really needed. As much as life sometimes got me down, I really liked living. I still do. As a child, I wanted to grow up. I wanted to have my own children. A gun could put a stop to that. So, I never touched it, and it stayed in its place, leaning against a closet wall in the utility room.

That was pretty much as far as gun safety went.

When I went to college, I learned that politically correct people don't like guns. I learned that guns were awful and evil and that I'd grown up in some kind of abusive home, supposedly, because our shotgun wasn't behind all those locks.

During my last semester of graduate school, I met the man who would become the father of my children. But there was the gun thing that I had to just accept about him. I didn't understand what he meant about all this guns-protecting-us-from-the-government stuff. Guns were for hunting, I reasoned, and if you have a license for a gun, then you should be happy, right? We didn't talk much about the gun thing for a while.

The Loss of Personal Freedoms

Our first son was not quite a year old when the September 11th tragedy occurred. While nursing his younger brother a couple of years later, I began to read on the Internet. I read about freedoms that I had thought I'd always have. I read about the loss of those freedoms, especially after September 11, 2001. I thought about how free we were, even as high school students, to make mistakes, to ride around town, to go through high school without signing a paper that says I have to agree to a random drug test if I want to participate in extracurricular activities.

Only a couple of decades later, a friend's daughter, who goes to a high school close to the one that my friend and I attended, must sign a paper saying that she'll agree to a random drug test. The closest town to where we grew up in North Carolina has banned cruising and signs tell you that you can now receive a ticket if you drive through town more than once; I noticed a similar sign near the ever-communist West Hollywood the other day. There is now zero tolerance for mistakes.

Things have definitely changed since I was in high school; freedoms are being lost faster than Confederate flags are being banned. People watch television and don't put up too much of a fight about these freedoms.

But what about guns? As I read more, I saw that Ruby Ridge, Waco, and other such tragedies, including the recent one in which several children were taken from their parents in Texas, are all about government control over people. The mainstream media make the victims of these things look crazy, and sometimes that's not hard to do, but the reality is that they are people who want to do their own thing while doing no harm to others. Why should the government care?

Self-Protection and the Constitution

The more I began to read, the more sense that guns made to me. Would I have to worry, for instance, about a Virginia Tech shooting scenario happening if I carried a gun? If someone came in a classroom with a gun and all the students were armed, how many students would a lone gunman be able to kill before he was killed? Could we not have avoided the campus lockdown thing and many deaths if guns had been encouraged on campus?

Besides the *gun* thing, there is the *other-parts-of-the-Constitution* thing. I'm beginning to understand now that many people are not into the Constitution these days; it's become somewhat passé in our current police state. Another homeschooling mom that I was talking to earlier this week seemed to think that I had a novel idea in citing the Fourth Amendment if a social wrecker comes to my door, asking to come in without a search warrant. Ah, the Constitution is great, when people remember it and apply it in their lives.

Here's what that wonderful document that men shed blood to write says about guns:

> A well regulated Militia, being necessary to the security of a free State, the right of the people to keep and bear Arms, shall not be infringed.

This kind of writing makes the gun permit that many of my friends and family in North Carolina hold so sacred seem silly. Why does anyone need a permit when the right to have a gun should *not be infringed*? Guns are powerful tools that allow us to defend ourselves and our families. Imagine how those who were alive during biblical times would have loved to have that kind of technology.

Protecting Oneself Against Government

I currently live in California, where even those who value the freedom of homeschooling often fail to value the freedom of having a gun. Or twelve. Or a hundred. All owned *sans* government control. Such a scenario scares far too many folks. Many people in the Southern end of the Golden State believe that guns cause problems and that the world will be a much better place when only government-deemed police officers are able to legally obtain guns. Most people don't think, although it could easily happen, that if the police break into your house in the middle of the night, a gun might protect you from them. Many people fail to see that if you're at a traffic light and someone carjacks you and your children, a gun might scare the would-be thief away much more easily than a scared and desperate call to a 9-1-1 dispatcher. Maybe the problem is that not many people think much about guns anymore; we simply accept what the government and mainstream media tell us.

What will happen to us as a society when we're completely unarmed and the only armed folks are police officers who have been well-trained by federal officials—as most police officers are these days—the federal officials who, ignoring California state law, for instance, come in and close down perfectly legal and thriving marijuana dispensaries? What will happen when federally-trained police officers, many of whom have been trained to kill in the unconstitutionally declared Iraq war, come to your door demanding your children, as officers did recently in Texas? Do guns look so terrible, so ominous, when these things occur? Does defending ourselves against an out-of-control government seem silly when that government is threatening your family?

Turns out, my husband was right about the gun thing. Although many people have a hard time understanding this idea, government works much better *when we are armed*, the way that our Founding Fathers intended it. An armed citizenry allows government to truly be *by the people*: Think about how much the government does what *you* want; then think about how many people walk around *unarmed* these days. The fewer armed citizens there are, the more powerful the government.

Gun Control
Is Not Acceptable

Aaron Zelman, interviewed by John F. McManus

Aaron Zelman is the executive director of Jews for the Preservation of Firearms Ownership (JPFO). He and his organization strongly believe in the eradication of all gun-control measures. In this interview Zelman explains why he is against any form of gun control. He says in countries like Turkey and China, past gun-control measures have left the population helpless against genocide. He also notes that in the United States, the 1968 Gun Control Act was based on an interpretation of gun laws from Nazi Germany. JPFO works to promote gun ownership and self-protection, publishing books like Dial 911 and Die *and supporting the Goody Guns project. In the Goody Guns project, cookie cutters are made in the shape of handguns to help children learn about gun safety. While Zelman believes that the media has been overly critical of JPFO, he and his organization remain committed to sponsoring the need for an armed citizenry. John F. Mc-Manus, who interviewed Zelman for* New American, *is the magazine's publisher.*

*T*HE NEW AMERICAN: *What is your organization's main goal?*

Aaron Zelman: Our main goal is to destroy gun control. We are an organization that believes we have the moral authority to point out to the rest of the world the evils that have come from gun control and how humanity has suffered because of gun-control schemes.

Are people who aren't Jewish members of your organization?

We have members of our organization that have told us they are not Jewish. We don't ask people what their religion is. And we are not an organization that is preaching religion to anybody.

We think the history of gun-control schemes has been so harmful to Jews that we have the moral authority to speak out. We welcome anybody who accepts the JPFO [Jews for the Preservation of Firearms Ownership] position that gun control must be destroyed.

We're not interested in compromise. We are only interested in the destruction of something we consider to be a very evil and deadly policy known as gun control.

How did you become involved in something like this?

Well, I've been involved in promoting gun ownership because of my family history to some degree. When my father was about six months old, his family had to leave the Ukraine in Russia because Stalin came to power. Stalin was not interested in kulaks owning land.

And so they lost everything they had, essentially, and fled to Canada where my dad was raised and served in the Canadian Army during World War II. So, I learned at a very, very early age what happens when you can't defend your life against a government gone bad.

Could you give us some examples of what has happened in other nations where gun control was in place?

Well, there are several. Why don't we start with the film we created called *Innocents Betrayed*? The film shows the history of and the connection between gun registration, confiscation, and how a police state is able to come about. It shows how the police state can target individuals they don't want to live and murder them—otherwise known as genocide.

Where has this happened?

Historically it happened in Turkey, known as the Armenian Genocide, and then, of course, in China, Russia, Germany, Cambodia, Rwanda, Uganda, and even now in Darfur.

You've actually obtained some of the documents from these different countries, and you've translated them so that we who read only English can read them?

A number of years ago we started this project of trying to find out if there was a connection among governments and if governments did the same thing. As we put it, these folks all go to the same dictators' school. Indeed, there is a connection because there is a pattern.

They realize they can't stay in power if the peasants have pitchforks and can march on the gates of the city. The way to bring about a dictatorship or police state is to make sure the people are disarmed.

I understand you have done work showing the source of the 1968 gun law here in the United States.

The 1968 Gun Control Act, as we know it today, became law during the [Lyndon] Johnson administration. The history behind the 1968 act is indeed fascinating.

The author of the federal Gun Control Act, Senator Thomas Dodd, was an attorney with the U.S. Justice Department at Nuremburg. He obtained the Reichsgesetzblatt, which is the German equivalent of our *Federal Register*. He was able to use the German gun-control laws after giving them to the Library of Congress to translate for him. They did indeed translate the laws for him, and that was the model, the basis, for the 1968 Gun Control Act in America.

Many Americans believe that it is the duty of police to protect them. Comment?

The police do not have a duty to protect individuals. The shield on the side of the car may say "to protect and serve," but the reality is, and by state law and the state statutes and case law, you do not have a right to police protection.

We have a book we publish entitled *Dial 911 and Die.* It's written by an attorney named Richard Stevens. The book details laws in every single state in the Union, the state statutes as well as case law, concerning calling 911.

You can sue the police if they fail to protect you, and your heirs can sue the police if you die during a criminal's attack on you, but you won't accomplish anything because the judge will finally tell you that there is no duty for the police to protect an individual unless there's been a prior agreement that they will offer you protection.

If you've been an informant for the police, if you are involved in some type of work for the police where the police are not able to protect you, if it's dangerous work, you are entitled. But short of that the police have no duty to protect you.

Could you tell us about "Goody Guns"?

Goody Guns is a program we started to save our children from the clutches of the gun prohibitionists in the public school system. Goody Guns are cookie cutters in the shape of revolvers or pistols, and the purpose of using them as you bake cookies for your children, or grandchildren, is to teach them firearm safety while they are eating their cookie.

You tell them to eat the cookie from the back of the gun where the handle is to the front of the gun where the muzzle is. And so they learn an important fact on firearms safety—controlling where the muzzle is pointed. You start early with the Goody Guns, and by the time they get to the public school system and they hear all the propaganda about guns being bad, they will know better.

When we first introduced Goody Guns, gun prohibitionists had a conniption fit because they knew the psychology behind our program. They realized they can't get into your home when the kid is two years old; they have to wait until your child is six years old in the school system, and by then they've lost.

Once Goody Guns went up on the Internet, everybody knew about it. We had, concerning Goody Guns, a call from a television station in England that was producing a program on guns in America. And they were curious about Goody Guns.

The person who called me wanted to know what the rationale behind Goody Guns was, and I sensed from the way she was asking the questions that she was trying to figure out a way to maneuver something to cause us a problem. Finally, she acknowledged, after we were almost done, that this was very clever and would probably be very effective. End of conversation. She put the phone down.

Have you been blasted by the media for this?

Well, the media is being true to form. They want to ignore anything that JPFO does. But the gun prohibitionists remain incensed. They had to speak out against it.

What's the greatest threat on the horizon right now for the right to keep and bear arms?

I think there are numerous threats, but one is that the American public really doesn't understand a need for an armed citizenry. Our country became independent because citizens were armed. This is why an organized, state-controlled militia received attention in the U.S. Constitution. So we have a lot of work to do.

We have to reach out to people and help them understand why citizens must be armed, and what's happened to citizens throughout the world and throughout history when they couldn't defend themselves against a government gone bad.

Organizations to Contact

The editors have compiled the following list of organizations concerned with the issues debated in this book. The descriptions are derived from materials provided by the organizations. All have publications or information available for interested readers. The list was compiled on the date of publication of the present volume; information provided here may change. Be aware that many organizations take several weeks or longer to respond to inquiries, so allow as much time as possible.

American Civil Liberties Union (ACLU)
125 Broad Street, 18th Floor, New York, NY   10004
(212) 549-2500 • fax: (212) 549-2646
E-mail: aclu@aclu.org
Web site: www.aclu.org

The ACLU is a national organization that defends Americans' civil rights as guaranteed in the U.S. Constitution. It advocates for freedom of all forms of speech, including pornography, flag burning, and political protest. The ACLU offers numerous reports, fact sheets, and policy statements on free speech issues, which are available on its Web site. Some of these publications include "Free Speech Under Fire," "Freedom of Expression," and, for students, "Ask Sybil Liberty About Your Right to Free Expression."

Cato Institute
1000 Massachusetts Ave. NW, Washington, DC   20001-5403
(202) 842-0200 • fax: (202) 842-3490
Web site: www.cato.org

The Cato Institute is a libertarian public-policy research foundation. It evaluates government policies and offers reform proposals and commentary on its Web site. Its publications include the Cato Policy Analysis series of reports, which have covered topics such as "Fighting Back: Crime, Self-Defense, and the Right to Carry a Handgun," and "Trust the People: The Case Against Gun Control." It also publishes the magazine *Regulation*, the *Cato Policy Report*, and books such as *The Samurai, the Mountie, and the Cowboy: Should America Adopt the Gun Controls of Other Democracies?*

Center to Prevent Handgun Violence
1225 Eye Street NW, Suite 1100, Washington, DC   20005
(202) 289-7319 • fax: (202) 408-1851
Web sites: www.cphv.org and www.gunlawsuits.com

The center is the legal action, research, and education affiliate of Handgun Control, Inc. The center's Legal Action Project provides free legal representation for victims in lawsuits against reckless gun manufacturers, dealers, and owners. The center's Straight Talk About Risks (STAR) program is a violence prevention program designed to help youth develop victim prevention skills and to rehearse behaviors needed to manage conflicts without violence or guns. The organization's Web sites provide fact sheets and updates on pending gun lawsuits.

Citizens Committee for the Right to Keep and Bear Arms
12500 NE Tenth Place, Bellevue, WA   98005
(425) 454-4911 • fax: (425) 451-3959
Web site: www.ccrkba.org

The committee believes that the U.S. Constitution's Second Amendment guarantees and protects the right of individual Americans to own guns. It works to educate the public concerning this right and to lobby legislators to prevent the passage of gun control laws. The committee is affiliated with the Second Amendment Foundation and has more than six hundred thousand members. It publishes the books *Gun Laws of America, Gun Rights Fact Book, Origin of the Second Amendment*, and *Point Blank: Guns and Violence in America*.

Coalition for Gun Control

P.O. Box 90062, 1488 Queen Street W
Toronto, Ontario   M6K 3K3
(416) 604-0209
Web site: www.guncontrol.ca

The coalition was formed to reduce gun death, injury, and crime. It supports the registration of all guns and works for tougher restrictions on handguns. The organization promotes safe-storage requirements for all firearms and educates to counter the romance of guns. Various fact sheets and other education materials on gun control are available on the organization's Web site.

Coalition to Stop Gun Violence

1023 15th Street NW, Suite 301, Washington, DC   20005
(202) 408-0061
Web site: www.csgv.org

The coalition lobbies at the local, state, and federal levels to ban the sale of handguns and assault weapons to individuals and to institute licensing and registration of all firearms. It also litigates cases against firearms makers. Its publications include various informational sheets on gun violence and the *Annual Citizens' Conference to Stop Gun Violence Briefing Book*, a compendium of gun control fact sheets, arguments, and resources.

Doctors for Responsible Gun Ownership

The Claremont Institute, 937 West Foothill Blvd., Suite E
Claremont, CA   91711
(909) 621-6825 • fax: (909) 626-8724
Web site: www.claremont.org

The organization is comprised of health professionals familiar with guns and medical research. It works to correct poor medical scholarship about the dangers of guns and to educate people on the importance of guns for self-defense. The organization has legally challenged laws that regulate guns. Its publications include the booklet *Firearms: A Handbook for Health Officials.*

Independence Institute

13952 Denver West Parkway, Suite 400, Golden, CO   80401
(303) 279-6536 • fax: (303) 279-4176
Web site: www.i2i.org

The Independence Institute is a pro-free-market think tank that supports gun ownership as a civil liberty and a constitutional right. Its publications include booklets opposing gun control, such as *Children and Guns: Sensible Solutions, "Shall Issue": The New Wave of Concealed Handgun Permit Laws,* and *Unfair and Unconstitutional: The New Federal Gun Control and Juvenile Crime Proposals,* as well as the book *Guns: Who Should Have Them?* The organization's Web site also contains articles, fact sheets, and commentary from a variety of sources.

Jews for the Preservation of Firearms Ownership (JPFO)

P.O. Box 270143, Hartford, WI   53207
(262) 673-9745 • fax: (262) 673-9746
Web site: www.jpfo.org

JPFO is an educational organization that believes Jewish law mandates self-defense. Its primary goal is the elimination of the idea that gun control is a socially useful public policy in any country. JPFO publishes the quarterly *Firearms Sentinel,* the booklet *Will "Gun Control" Make You Safer?,* and regular news alerts.

Million Mom March Foundation

1225 Eye Street NW, Suite 1100, Washington, DC   20005
(888) 989-MOMS • fax: (202) 408-1851
e-mail: national@millionmommarch.org
Web site: www.millionmommarch.org

The foundation is a grassroots organization that supports commonsense gun laws. The foundation organized the Million Mom March, in which thousands marched through Washington, D.C., on Mother's Day, May 14, 2000, in support of licensing and registration and other firearms regulations. The foundation's Web site provides fact sheets on gun violence and gun control initiatives.

National Crime Prevention Council (NCPC)
2345 Crystal Drive, Suite 500, Arlington, VA   22202
(800) 851-3420
Web site: www.ncpc.org

The NCPC is a branch of the U.S. Department of Justice. Through its programs and education materials, the council works to teach Americans how to reduce crime and to address its causes. It provides readers with information on gun control and gun violence. NCPC's publications include the newsletter *Catalyst,* which is published ten times a year, and the book *Reducing Gun Violence: What Communities Can Do.*

National Criminal Justice Reference Service (NCJRS)
Box 6000, Rockville, MD   20849-6000
(301) 519-3420
Web site: www.ncjrs.org

A component of the Office of Justice Programs of the U.S. Department of Justice, the NCJRS supports research on crime, criminal behavior, and crime prevention and serves as a clearinghouse for information. Its publications include the research briefs "Reducing Youth Gun Violence: An Overview of Programs and Initiatives," "Impacts of the 1994 Assault Weapons Ban," and "Homicide in Eight U.S. Cities: Trends, Context, and Policy Implications."

National Rifle Association of America (NRA)
11250 Waples Mill Road, Fairfax, VA   22030
(800) 672-3888
Web site: www.nra.org

With nearly three million members, the NRA is America's largest organization of gun owners. It is also the primary lobbying group for those who oppose gun control laws. The NRA believes that such laws violate the U.S. Constitution and do nothing to reduce crime. In addition to its monthly magazines *America's 1st Freedom, American Rifleman, American Hunter, Insights,* and *Shooting Sports USA,* the NRA publishes numerous books, bibliographies, reports, and pamphlets on gun ownership, gun safety, and gun control.

Second Amendment Foundation

12500 NE Tenth Place, Bellevue, WA   98005
(425) 454-7012 • fax: (425) 451-3959
Web site: www.saf.org

The foundation is dedicated to informing Americans about their Second Amendment right to keep and bear firearms. It believes that gun control laws violate this right. The foundation publishes numerous books, including *The Amazing Vanishing Second Amendment, The Best Defense: True Stories of Intended Victims Who Defended Themselves with a Firearm,* and *CCW: Carrying Concealed Weapons.* The complete text of the book *How to Defend Your Gun Rights* is available on its Web site.

U.S. Department of Justice

Office of Justice Programs, Washington, DC   20530-0001
(202) 514-2000
Web site: www.usdoj.gov

The Department of Justice protects citizens by maintaining effective law enforcement, crime prevention, crime detection, and prosecution and rehabilitation of offenders. Through its Office of Justice Programs, the department operates the National Institute of Justice, the Office of Juvenile Justice and Delinquency Prevention, and the Bureau of Justice Statistics. Its publications include fact sheets, research packets, bibliographies, and the semiannual journal *Juvenile Justice.*

Violence Policy Center

1730 Rhode Island Ave. NW, Suite 1014
Washington, DC   20036

(202) 822-8200
Web site: www.vpc.org

The center is an educational foundation that conducts research on firearms violence. It works to educate the public
concerning the dangers of guns and supports gun control
measures. The center's publications include the reports *Handgun Licensing and Registration: What it Can and Cannot Do,
Gunland USA: A State-by-State Ranking of Gun Shows, Gun
Retailers, Machine Guns, and Gun Manufacturers*, and *Guns for
Felons: How the NRA Works to Rearm Criminals.*

For Further Research

Books

Massad Ayoob, *The Truth About Self-Protection*. Concord, NH: Police Bookshelf, March 2004.

Kyle Cassidy, *Armed America: Portraits of Gun Owners in Their Homes*. Fairfield, OH: Krause, 2007.

Philip J. Cook and Jens Ludwig, *Gun Violence: The Real Costs*. New York: Oxford University Press, 2002.

Saul Cornell, *A Well-Regulated Militia: The Founding Fathers and the Origins of Gun Control in America*. New York: Oxford University Press, 2006.

Alan Gottlieb and Dave Workman, *America Fights Back: Armed Self-Defense in a Violent Age*. Bellevue, WA: Merril Press, 2007.

David Hemenway, *Private Guns, Public Health*. Ann Arbor: University of Michigan Press, 2004.

James B. Jacobs, *Can Gun Control Work?* New York: Oxford University Press, 2004.

Gary Kleck, *Point Blank: Guns and Violence in America*. Piscataway, NJ: Aldine Transaction, 2005.

Gary Kleck and Don B. Kates, *Armed: New Perspectives on Gun Control*. Amherst, NY: Prometheus Books, 2001.

Abigail A. Kohn, *Shooters: Myths and Realities of America's Gun Cultures*. New York: Oxford University Press, 2004.

Wayne LaPierre, *The Global War on Your Guns: Inside the UN Plan to Destroy the Bill of Rights*. Nashville, TN: Nelson Current, 2006.

Jens Ludwig and Philip J. Cook, eds., *Evaluating Gun Policy: Effects on Crime and Violence*. Washington, DC: Brookings Institution Press, 2003.

Joyce Lee Malcolm, *Guns and Violence: The English Experience*. Cambridge, MA: Harvard University Press, 2004.

Fumio Matsuo, *Democracy with a Gun: America and the Policy of Force*. Berkeley, CA: Stone Bridge, 2007.

Andrew J. McClurg, David B. Kopel, and Brannon P. Denning, eds., *Gun Control and Gun Rights: A Reader and Guide*. New York: New York University Press, 2002.

Chris McNab and Hunter Keeter, *Tools of Violence: Guns, Tanks, and Dirty Bombs*. New York: Osprey, 2008.

Jeffrey D. Monroe, *Homicide and Gun Control: The Brady Handgun Violence Prevention Act and Homicide Rates*. El Paso, TX: LFB Scholarly, 2008.

Mark Progrebin, *Guns, Violence, and Criminal Behavior: The Offender's Perspective*. Boulder, CO: Lynne Rienner, 2009.

Robert J. Spitzer, *The Politics of Gun Control*, 3rd ed. Washington, DC: CQ Press, 2003.

Articles

America, "The World Is Watching," May 14, 2007.

Capital Times, "Timid Congress Forces Mayors to Move on Guns," May 1, 2006, A8.

Hector Castro, "Police Chief Reacts to Shootings: He Cites Easy Access to Guns, Limited Mental Health Care," *Seattle Post-Intelligencer*, April 25, 2006, B1.

Christian Science Monitor, "Is Self-Defense Law Vigilante Justice? Some Say Proposed Laws Can Help Deter Gun Violence. Others Worry About Deadly Confrontations," February 4, 2006, 2.

Crime Control Digest, "Boston Opens Center to Curb Gun Violence," November 4, 2005.

Crime Control Digest, "Connecticut Hits Guns in Anti-Violence Drive," February 24, 2006.

Kenneth Epps, "Addressing Small Arms Violence in the Caribbean," *Ploughshares Monitor*, Summer 2008.

Sarah Fulford, "I'm No Longer Surprised When Someone Is Shot Dead on Our Streets," *Toronto Life*, August 2008.

Shirley Henderson, "A Shooter's Story," *Ebony*, July 2008.

Shirley Henderson, "Parents Find Purpose in Their Pain; Our Children Didn't Die in Vain," *Ebony*, July 2008.

Dan C. Johnson, "Basic Manly Skills," *Handguns*, June–July 2007.

Mike Kennedy, "Responding to Tragedy," *American School and University*, April 1, 2004.

Wayne LaPierre, "Let's Outlaw Illegal Guns," *American Rifleman*, June 2009.

"Put the Guns Down," *Maclean's*, April 30, 2007.

David E. Petzal, "Is Your Gun Happy?" *Field and Stream*, June 2007.

Natalie Pompilio, "Every Day of the Year, Somebody's Getting Killed," *Philadelphia Inquirer*, May 2, 2006.

Jeff Snyder, "Violence and Nonviolence: Part 1," *American Handgunner*, September 1, 2005, 80(4).

Jeff Snyder, "Violence and Nonviolence: Part 2," *American Handgunner*, March 1, 2006, 92(3).

Jeff Snyder, "Violence and Nonviolence: Part 3," *American Handgunner*, May 1, 2006, 82(4).

"A Law Full of Holes," *Star-Ledger (Newark, NJ)*, March 19, 2006, 3.

Tabatha Wethal, "Painting the Nation's Arms Neon: Are Brightly Colored Firearms Putting Officers in Danger?" *Law Enforcement Technology*, May 2008.

Kurt Williamsen, "Exercising the Right," *New American*, May 26, 2008.

Index